Preparing

Preparing to Preach

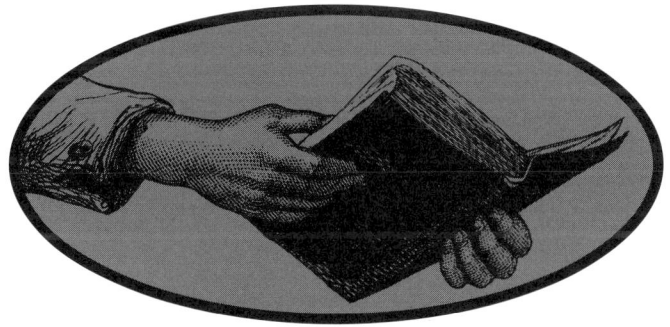

**A Practical Guide
for
Beginning Preachers**

Bill D. Whittaker

PROVIDENCE HOUSE PUBLISHERS
Franklin, Tennessee

Copyright 1999 by Bill D. Whittaker

All rights reserved. Written permission must be secured from the publisher to use or reproduce any part of this book, except for brief quotations in critical reviews or articles.

Printed in the United States of America

03   02   01   00   99   1   2   3   4   5

Library of Congress Catalog Card Number: 99-64289

ISBN: 1-57736-150-4

Cover design by Gary Bozeman

PROVIDENCE HOUSE PUBLISHERS
238 Seaboard Lane • Franklin, Tennessee 37067
800-321-5692
www.providencehouse.com

To the

Glory of God

And in Thanksgiving for

Rebecca

John and Jessica

Karen and Darrin

Mary, G. L., and Kaela

Contents

Preface		ix
Introduction		xi
Unit 1	PREACHING THEN AND NOW	3
1	What Is Preaching?	5
2	New Testament Sermons	11
3	Why Preaching Today?	18
Unit 2	PREPARING THE PREACHER	23
4	Who Qualifies?	25
5	The Preacher's Authority	31
6	Excuses for Inadequate Preparation	36
Unit 3	UNDERSTANDING THE WORD	43
7	Where Does He Find Those Great Ideas?	45
8	A Text for the Sermon	53
9	Interpreting the Text	59
Unit 4	ORGANIZING THE MESSAGE	71
10	Preaching Objectives	73
11	Maintaining Unity in the Sermon	78
12	Body Building	82
13	Sermon Structure	88
14	"In Conclusion"	96
15	Introduction, Please	106
Unit 5	PUTTING LIGHT ON THE TRUTH	113
16	The Text and Life Application	115

	17	Illustrating the Sermon	122
	18	Just Imagine	136
Unit 6	SERMON WORKSHOP		141
	19	Evangelistic Preaching	143
	20	Doctrinal Preaching	152
	21	Ethical Preaching	159
	22	Pastoral Preaching	165
Unit 7	MAKING THE MOST OF PREPARATION		177
	23	Planning Your Preaching	179
	24	Retaining Resources and Recycling Results	185

Endnotes	193
Bibliography	201
Clear Creek Baptist Bible College	205
Biblical Reference Index	209
About the Author	211

Preface

As a student pastor I often delayed sermon preparation and then hoped for a "Saturday night miracle." I frequently went to the pulpit with a baptized version of William Barclay's New Testament comments. Then I discovered the excitement of first encountering God's truth before seeking other ideas. I returned to my calling. Since the Lord called me to preach, He would lead me in preparing to preach.

Each time a preacher is asked to preach, a spiritual battle is fought again. Will you trust the Lord for the message? Will you work with Him to prepare the message? God called you to preach. Will you invest adequate time in prayer, Bible study, and sermon preparation?

The absolute trustworthiness of the Word of God undergirds this text. Three decades of preaching have deepened my love for the Bible and secured my faith in its message. I share the testimony of English preacher Charles Simeon, "I love the simplicity of the Scriptures, . . . I soon learn that I must take the Scriptures with the simplicity of a little child and be content to receive on God's testimony what He has revealed, whether I can unravel all the difficulties that may attend it or not."

The best sermons possess a practical dimension, and homiletics ought to be practical. One student, aware of my writing this volume, strongly recommended, "Make it basic!" There is a place for the theology and philosophy of preaching, but a beginning preacher yearns for practicality. This text began among practical needs on the mission field. In the Philippines I taught beginning preachers at a Bible institute. Many of the students were pastors of newly organized churches or led Bible study groups with the goal of planting churches. I wrote a textbook for the Theological Education by Extension program for use by small groups of preachers gathered to study in the setting of local ministry. "Make it practical, with plenty of 'how-to-do-it' suggestions," the editor emphasized. That volume has now gone into a second printing.

Back in America I felt the need for a similar text to use with beginning preachers in the Bible college setting. A class of 32, most of them "beginners," affirmed the need for a practical approach. This volume reflects the shared experience of that class and several others.

I am indebted to many for encouragement in this project. Former academic dean and English professor Daryls Warren and preaching professor Robert Oldham provided helpful evaluations and suggestions. Bible instructor John Ditty "field-tested" an edition, and improvements came from him and the students. I am very grateful for my secretary, Mrs. Shelby Castlen, for preparation of the manuscript.

I thank God for the encouragement of my wife, Rebecca, and for her partnership in His work. A special thanks to the trustee executive committee and Dr. and Mrs. Dudley Pomeroy for support in this project. Dr. Pomeroy was a long-time pastor, army chaplain, and Clear Creek professor. After his retirement, he was elected to the board of trustees. Proceeds from the sale of this book provide funds for the Jean Asher and Dudley Pomeroy Scholarship for the benefit of ministry students at Clear Creek Baptist Bible College.

Bill D. Whittaker
2 Thessalonians 5:16-18

Introduction

It didn't matter to Archie Oliver that his first opportunity to preach was in a small country church; this was a big opportunity and the beginning of his ministry. He worked hard on the message and thought he had enough material to preach twenty to thirty minutes. When he finished, eight minutes had elapsed. Length never determines the quality of preaching, nor how the Lord will use it. "The best part of that experience came during the invitation when two young men trusted the Lord Jesus," Oliver vividly remembers.

Archie Oliver could have kept on preaching in the same manner with the rationalization, "I can do it and people get saved; what more do I need?" However, Archie realized that his calling included the calling to prepare, and, as a married man, he made the commitment to train at our Bible college. The experience whetted his appetite for more, and his forty-six-year preaching ministry has included many seminars, correspondence courses, and other study opportunities.

How one begins can make all the difference in a lifetime of preaching. Some evaluate their beginning unsuccessfully and decide "God didn't really call me." However, the Lord may be growing our patience, helping us to walk by faith and trust His sovereign will and the power of His Word. One young preacher's beginning was marked with unusual numbers of public decisions, and a small church quickly grew. The pastor decided he didn't need any training; the Lord had laid on him the power and gift of preaching. The following years were not so successful. I often pondered what difference might have been made had he gained additional study skills, had the exposure to experienced teachers, dialogued and prayed with fellow students, and faced the suggestions and evaluation of his peers.

This study begins with a look at the nature of preaching and its relevance today. Since preaching involves a preacher, you need to examine your calling, authority, and commitment to quality preparation. The major portion of our study focuses on understanding a text, gathering materials, and finding a way of presenting the message. Specific attention spotlights four kinds of sermons: evangelistic, doctrinal, ethical, pastoral. The last unit looks at how to plan your preaching, use the computer, and get maximum use from the work of preparing a sermon.

Many of the lessons include "Reaction and Response" opportunities for additional study. The Lord teaches us by a variety of ways, and we can learn even from those with whom we disagree on some issues. Unless otherwise stated, Scripture references are from the New King James Version.

Am I wrong to assume that your use of this book indicates a commitment to the work needed to "rightly divide the word of truth"? Time will tell. Others have only wanted to "pass the course." A preacher's final grade comes from the One who called us. In the interim, we keep on preparing to preach.

Preparing to Preach

Unit 1

Preaching Then and Now

I recall a news story about a federal office building that underwent extensive and expensive renovation within a year of the building dedication. The contractor cut corners on the foundation. Biblical preaching rests on the foundation of truth revealed in Scripture. Unit One examines some basic Scriptures that help you understand the nature of preaching and start you on the task of laying a theological foundation for the practical aspects of sermon preparation. There are excellent contemporary examples for Biblical preaching, but we must not ignore the New Testament models. Jesus, Peter, Stephen, Philip, and Paul offer crucial characteristics for preaching today.

Why do we preach today? Chapter three considers four reasons for the necessity of preaching in our time. God's preacher must be convinced of the significance that preaching has in God's plan. Paul, writing about church worship and spiritual gifts, used the analogy of a trumpet. "For if the trumpet makes an uncertain sound, who will prepare for battle?" (1 Cor. 14:8). In preaching, God's messenger sounds the trumpet and calls people to prepare. Uncertainty weakens the message, betrays the call, and leaves the listener more vulnerable to the enemy.

A biblical preacher who faithfully fulfills the mandate of Christ continues the heritage of the early church and can expect to hear Christ's commendation.

Chapter 1
What Is Preaching?

What happened in your church last Sunday? Recall the different events of the worship service. The following probably occurred: music, prayers, welcome to visitors, announcements, testimony, preaching, and invitation. Which one of these took the most time? Most likely, preaching. In most evangelical churches, the sermon is the main part of the service. Every pastor preaches regularly, sometimes two or three times a week, to the same group of people. The people expect to hear a good message. God wants His message to be heard and people to follow His will.

As a major responsibility of every pastor, preaching deserves the best preparation of which he is capable. This book is written to help you understand more about biblical preaching and to learn some principles of sermon preparation. This task begins with a look at several Bible passages which help you understand the nature of preaching.

What is preaching? Before you read any further, write out a definition for preaching. At the close of this lesson we will examine some definitions written by other beginning preachers and determine how your description compares.

A DEFINITION OF BIBLICAL PREACHING

The Bible does not provide a formal definition of preaching, but it does say much about preaching. Two Greek words provide additional understanding of the nature of preaching. The most common Greek word in the New Testament for preaching is *kerussein*. It is translated as "preach" fifty-three times and as "publish" five times.

5

Kerussein means "to make proclamation as a herald." A herald was a public messenger who lifted up his voice and called public attention to some news he desired to announce. The herald's job was very important in the days before the printing press, radio, or television. In the public square, the herald would cry out the news or events affecting people's lives. The herald needed a strong voice and sometimes used a trumpet. The herald had to deliver the message exactly as it was given to him.

The Old Testament has some examples of the herald. Pharoah ordered heralds to go in front of Joseph's chariot, crying out, "Bow the knee!" (Gen. 41:43). King Nebuchadnezzar sent a herald to proclaim his order for all men to "worship the gold image" (Dan. 3:1–5). Among the prophets, *kerussein* is often connected with a national crisis and a "sense of urgency." Joel proclaimed an assembly before the coming day of the Lord (1:14, 2:15), and Hosea called for proclamation to be made (5:8). The prophets linked joy with urgency and looked forward to the coming of God's Servant who would usher in the kingdom of God. The herald's proclamation would be fulfilled in Jesus.[1]

Kerussein described the ministry of John the Baptist, the forerunner of Jesus. "In those days John the Baptist came, preaching in the wilderness of Judea" (Matt. 3:1). This word was also used of Jesus. "From that time on Jesus began to preach" (Matt. 4:17). Both Jesus and John were heralds.

Another New Testament word is *euaggelizo*; it means "to tell the good news or good tidings." The noun translates as "gospel" or good news. *Euaggelizo* means to share the gospel and focuses on the message that is preached. The herald of God does not preach just any message. God's messenger proclaims the "good news." The preacher shares the gospel of Jesus Christ.

When some people tried to keep Jesus in their area, he responded, "I must preach the kingdom of God to the other cities also, because for this purpose I have been sent" (Luke 4:43). The ministry of Jesus was summarized, "Jesus went about all Galilee, teaching in their synagogues, preaching the gospel of the kingdom, and healing all kinds of sickness and all kinds of disease among the people" (Matt. 4:23). This verse, along with other references, points out the close relation between "preaching" and "teaching." Jesus' inaugural sermon in Nazareth reflects his teaching them the meaning of his proclamation.[2]

Public preaching of the good news of Jesus was the first work of the apostles. The disciple, Peter, said God "commanded us to preach" (Acts 10:42). The apostles obeyed that command—"they did not cease teaching and preaching Jesus is the Christ" (Acts 5:42).

Others in the church also preached the gospel. Philip was a dedicated deacon in the early church, and the Lord gave him many opportunities to preach. He "went down to the city of Samaria and preached (*kerussein*) Christ

What Is Preaching?

to them" (Acts 8:5). Many of the people "believed Philip as he preached (*kerussein*) the good news (*euaggelizo*) of the kingdom of God and the name of Jesus Christ" (Acts 8:12 NIV).

Paul wrote that Christ sent him to "preach (*kerussein*) the gospel (*euaggelizo*)" (1 Cor. 1:17).

Kerussein is the proclamation of a herald or messenger; *euaggelizo* is telling the good news. When these two words are united, a definition of preaching begins to form. Preaching is the proclamation of the good news of Jesus Christ by a person chosen of God. Notice our definition has two main parts: first, a person chosen by God who proclaims (preaches); and second, a message of the good news of Jesus Christ.

Biblical preaching includes a third part. Preaching calls for a response from the hearer. The proclamation includes asking people to do something. The messenger asks the listener to decide. Look again at Scripture references with the two key words for preaching:

> Matt. 4:17—Jesus preached and asked the people to "repent, for the kingdom of heaven is at hand." His hearers had to decide to turn away from sin and believe in Christ.

> Acts 8:12—". . . they believed Philip as he preached the good news." The people made a personal decision of trust following Philip's preaching.

> 1 Cor. 1:21—"It pleased God through the foolishness of the message preached to save those who believe." This verse teaches that God will give new life to all who respond with faith to the preaching of the gospel.

Throughout the New Testament, preaching involves the listeners in making a decision about the message, as well as exhorting them to Christian growth in grace.

The biblical preacher preaches for a decision, but the conversion decision is only the beginning. Biblical preaching also calls the people of God to maturity in Christ, to service, and to love. These responses may not always be made known in a public decision.

Paul, writing in 2 Corinthians 5:18–20, stressed the important position of the person who shares the good news:

> Now all things are of God, who has reconciled us to himself through Jesus Christ and has given us the ministry of reconciliation: that is that God was reconciling the world to himself, not imputing their trespasses to them, and

has committed to us the word of reconciliation. Now then, we are ambassadors for Christ, as though God were pleading through us, we implore you on Christ's behalf, be reconciled to God.

Frequently, the nation's president will receive an ambassador from another country. The ambassador will present his credentials to the president. The ambassador represents his government to this country; the government speaks through its ambassador. Every Christian is an ambassador for Christ. We represent Him in the world; we speak "on Christ's behalf." If we do not preach His message, the world will not hear. Paul asked, "how shall they hear without a preacher?" (Rom. 10:14).

The preacher appeals on behalf of Christ. Biblical preaching must include the urgent plea to accept the good news of Christ. The urgency arises from personal awareness of having been "reconciled . . . through Christ." The peace and joy of a new relationship must be communicated with others.

Urgent desire seizes the preacher because the eternal destiny of the hearers is involved. Paul urged, "we implore you." The same word describes the Gadarene demoniac who begged Jesus not to be tormented (Luke 8:28) and, following his conversion, begged to go with Him (Luke 8:38). Biblical preaching must include an urgent appeal.

We now have three parts in our definition of preaching:

1. A person representing Christ who preaches;
2. A message of the good news of Jesus Christ;
3. An urgent appeal for the hearers to decide.

A definition of preaching which includes these biblical concepts would be **the proclamation of the good news of Jesus by one representing Christ, urgently appealing for the hearers to respond positively to the will of God.**

With this definition as our guideline, let's evaluate some definitions written by other beginning preachers. Try to make your own evaluation before you read mine.

a. "Preaching is telling the message of God from the Bible."

This statement could describe the activity of a non-Christian. Preaching is the work of "one representing Christ." The Bible includes many messages of God. It is possible to preach a message from the Bible and it not be "the good news of Jesus." The statement also said nothing about the results. Biblical preaching asks "the hearers to respond positively to the will of God."

What Is Preaching?

b. "Preaching is the deliverance of a message which talks about God."

This definition says nothing about the messenger nor the urgent appeal for a decision. "A message which talks about God" can be only religious talk, saying nothing about Jesus nor giving any "good news" for the problems of people.

c. "Preaching is interpreting a text from the Bible to tell the people about the will of God."

All three parts of our definition are left out of this definition.

d. "Preaching is a communication to other persons so that the good news of Jesus may be known."

The Christianity of this proclaimer may be assumed by this statement. Preaching must be more than making known the good news. Preaching "urgently" appeals for the people to accept God's will in Christ.

e. "Preaching is speaking with a congregation about a certain topic and then discussing it."

This could define any public speech. It says nothing about the messenger, the good news of Jesus, and the urgent appeal for a decision.

Now study closely the definition you wrote at the outset of this lesson and compare it to the guideline. Should yours be rewritten? If so, write your revised definition here:

_____

_____

_____

Recall again the definition of preaching which includes all three biblical concepts. Biblical preaching is the proclamation of the good news of Jesus by one representing Jesus Christ, urgently appealing for the hearers to respond positively to the will of God. Preaching is a great responsibility; eternal life and death are involved in the hearers' response to the good news. The hard work needed to prepare to preach should be gladly assumed. Every effort to preach more effectively will have the blessing of Christ.

REACTION AND RESPONSE

Additional material on *euaggelizo* and *kerussein* and related words can be found in *Theological Dictionary of the New Testament*, abridged in one volume, by Geoffrey W. Bromiley (Grand Rapids: Wm. B. Eerdmans Publishing Co., 1985), 267–272, 430–435.

Read Ian Macpherson "The Burden," *The Burden of the Lord* (New York: Abingdon, 1955), 9–44.

Chapter 2
New Testament Sermons

To understand the nature of biblical preaching we can study sermons recorded in the New Testament. Only a few of the many sermons preached by Jesus and the first disciples are in the New Testament, but the Holy Spirit directed that these be recorded. These New Testament sermons are examples for today's preacher and tell us much about biblical preaching. If the basic characteristics of New Testament preaching are not in our messages, how can our sermons be called biblical?

THE PREACHING OF JESUS

According to Raymond Bailey, "Jesus provides the perfect professional role model for the pastor-preacher. His life revealed to us how to be persons, but it also disclosed how to do ministry."[1]

The first written record of Jesus' ministry gives a summary of his preaching: "Jesus came into Galilee, preaching the gospel of God, the kingdom, and saying 'The time is fulfilled, and the kingdom of God at hand. Repent and believe in the gospel'" (Mark 1:14–15). Jesus preached the good news. He was the good news! He declared, as a herald from heaven, the message of life in Himself. He announced the arrival of the King and the opportunity for others to be part of the kingdom of God.

Jesus' Sermon on the Mount, recorded in Matthew 5–7, is a sermon which describes life in the kingdom of God. He shared the good news of blessings in the kingdom of heaven, and boldly proclaimed the responsibilities of one in the kingdom. His gospel was contrasted with what "you have heard" (Matt. 5:21, 33, 38, 43). He preached something new—good news. This good news centered in Jesus, the King and Lord.

The Sermon on the Mount is a message about sin: murder and unjust anger (5:21–22), adultery and lust (6:25–34), worry (6:25–34), judging (7:1–2), hypocrisy (7:3–5). Jesus was honest about sin and the need for people to turn away from sin.

Jesus preached the meaning of Scripture and applied it to life needs. An experience Jesus had in His hometown of Nazareth shows His use of Scripture in preaching (Luke 4:16–30). His message in the synagogue was taken from Isaiah 61. He proclaimed the inspired Word of God. The people liked His message at first. "All spoke well of Him and were amazed at the gracious words that came from His lips" (4:22 NIV). Their support soon turned to hate when Jesus preached God's love to all people, i.e., to Gentiles as well as Jews, using Old Testament Scriptures to support His message. The Jewish listeners, who did not accept non-Jews, ran Jesus out of town and tried to kill Him. He honestly preached the meaning of Scripture and applied it to the needs of people without fear of their reaction.

Jesus asked His hearers to decide. He faced them with a decision to put God first—"seek first the kingdom of God and His righteousness" (Matt. 6:33). He offered the choice of the broad way which ends in destruction or the narrow way which leads to life (Matt. 7:13–14).

Jesus asked His hearers to respond positively to the will of God. "Repent and believe in the gospel" was Jesus' appeal (Mark 1:15). The Lord warned about substituting religious practices for God's way into the kingdom, "Not everyone who says to me, 'Lord, Lord,' shall enter the kingdom of heaven" (Matt. 7:21). Those who do His will enter the kingdom.

The Sermon on the Mount concludes with an illustration of two home builders (Matt. 7:24–27). The wise builder constructed his house upon the rock, and the house stood during the storm. The wise man is an example of the person who hears Jesus' message, the good news, and obeys the will of God.

The ministry of Jesus reveals these four characteristics of His preaching:

1. Jesus preached the good news of God, found in Himself.
2. Jesus honestly faced the problem of sin.
3. Jesus used Scripture and applied it to life needs.
4. Jesus asked people to decide, i.e., to obey God.

THE PREACHING OF THE FIRST CHURCH LEADERS

The New Testament book of Acts tells the story of the early church after Jesus returned to heaven. It was written by Luke who also wrote the third gospel. Acts records several sermons preached by the apostles and other church leaders. Their messages show they learned how to preach from Jesus.

THE PREACHING OF PETER

At the time of the Jewish religious festival Pentecost, the Holy Spirit was poured out upon the church (Acts 2). This event happened as Jesus promised (Acts 1:4–5). The Holy Spirit was given so the church would have power to witness and serve. "You shall receive power when the Holy Spirit has come upon you; and you shall be witnesses to me" (1:8).

The first powerful work of the Holy Spirit was to use the Jerusalem church members in witnessing to the large crowd of Jews present for the Pentecost festival. The Holy Spirit made it possible for the Christians to witness in the different languages those pilgrims spoke (xenoglasia). More than twelve different languages were present. Of course, the people were "amazed and perplexed" and began to ask, "What ever could this mean?" (2:12). Peter, the leader of the disciples, "raised his voice and spoke to the crowd." Peter's sermon (Acts 2:14–40) is an excellent example of first-century preaching.

Notice Peter started where the people were. The people questioned the language miracle, and some accused the disciples of drunkenness. Peter answered the charge and used it as a beginning point to explain the miracle. The Old Testament prophet Joel was quoted as a scriptural explanation for the events just seen. Peter used other Scriptures in his sermon: Psalm 16 (Acts 2:25–28) and Psalm 110:1 (vv. 34–35). Like Jesus, Peter preached the inspired Scriptures and applied them to the life situation.

Peter's sermon focused on Jesus. Jesus' life (v. 22), death (v. 23), resurrection (vv. 24, 32), and heavenly ascension (v. 33) were proclaimed to the crowd. Peter preached the lordship of Jesus Christ. "Therefore let all the house of Israel know assuredly that God has made this Jesus, whom you crucified, both Lord and Christ" (v. 36).

The apostle's message included the subject of sin. Peter boldly told the crowd, "you, have taken by lawless hands, have crucified, and put to death" (v. 23). "Repent . . . for the remission of sins" (v. 38). Peter described the people's relationship to God as those "who are far off" (v. 39). Without Christ they were lost, dead in sin, far away from God. Peter compassionately urged them to "Be saved from this perverse generation" (v. 40).

God used this message about personal sin and the need to trust Jesus to convince the hearers of their need. The people were "cut to the heart" and asked what to do (v. 37).

Peter continued to preach the good news when he offered forgiveness of sin to all who would repent. "With many other words he warned them; and he pleaded with them" (v. 40 NIV). Peter asked for a decision. He urgently appealed for the crowd to accept the gospel. Three thousand "received his word" and were baptized!

Acts includes another sermon preached by Peter in a different setting. Acts 10:34–43 contains a sermon delivered in the house of the Roman soldier, Cornelius. Most of the crowd were Gentiles, and Jewish law forbade a Jew to closely associate with Gentiles. Peter's sermon began with his personal testimony "that God shows no partiality. But in every nation whoever fears him and practices righteousness is accepted by him" (vv. 34–35). This gained the respect of his Gentile hearers and probably made them listen more closely.

Peter declared the good news of "peace through Jesus Christ, He is Lord of all" (v. 36). He reminded these seekers of Jesus' life (vv. 37–38), death (v. 39), and resurrection (vv. 40–41). Peter presented Jesus as the Judge of all mankind (v. 42). Sixteen times in these few verses a reference is made to Jesus. The eyes of the people were on Peter the preacher, but Peter turned their attention to Jesus.

No specific Scripture is quoted in the message, but Peter referred to the Old Testament when he said, "To Him [Jesus] the prophets witness" (v. 43). We do not know if the Holy Spirit moved Luke to write the full message or a condensation.

Although his hearers had a different background than the crowd in Jerusalem, Peter issued the same invitation to decide. "Whoever who believes in Him will receive remission of sins" (v. 43). All persons, Jews and Gentiles, are sinners; all need to repent and believe the good news. Only through the name of Jesus can people find forgiveness of sin. Peter preached about sin and the good news of salvation. Peter's preaching includes these characteristics:

1. Scripture was used and applied to life needs.
2. The message was good news about Jesus.
3. Sin was honestly faced.
4. The people were asked to obey God.

THE PREACHING OF LAY LEADERS

The Jerusalem church selected Stephen and Philip as lay leaders. Their first and primary job assignment involved food distribution among the widows. These two men realized that every Christian is an ambassador of Christ, so they also preached as the Lord provided opportunities.

Stephen's boldness resulted in arrest and death. Acts 7:2–53 contains his message before the Jewish Sanhedrin (high court). The listeners were religious leaders with much knowledge about the Old Testament, so Stephen began where they were with a review of God's work with the Israelites. He quoted from Old Testament Scripture (7:2–38). He reminded the Sanhedrin of Israel's disobedience (v. 39) and idolatry (vv. 40–43).

Sounding like the prophets he had quoted, Stephen said: "You stiff-necked people . . . you are just like your fathers: You always resist the Holy Spirit!" (v. 51 NIV). Stephen charged them with killing "The Righteous One," Jesus, and disobeying the law they claimed to have received (vv. 52–53). When Stephen declared he saw Jesus in glory, the crowd became furious. They "cast him out of the city and stoned him" (v. 58).

Stephen was unable to finish his message. The offer to turn from sin to Jesus and accept Christ's forgiveness was aborted. The crowd had made their decision before Stephen preached (Acts 6: 9–14). They listened only to find a place to express their rejection. Stephen's last words were a prayer for his killers, "Lord, do not charge them with this sin" (v. 60). His forgiving spirit and courageous death offered proof of the faith he had in the gospel he preached and the Lord he followed.

Persecution against the Jerusalem Christians erupted after Stephen's death. Many Christian disciples fled the city, including Philip. He "went down to the city of Samaria and preached the Christ to them" (Acts 8:5). None of Philip's sermons are written in Acts, but the content of his preaching is described. "Philip . . . preached the good news of the kingdom of God and the name of Jesus Christ" (8:12 NIV). His listeners believed the gospel; they made a decision in response to his invitation (8:12). Philip's encounter with the Ethiopian official also revealed him to be a preacher familiar with the Scriptures (Acts 8:26–34).

Stephen and Philip were courageous and faithful lay leaders who gladly preached the gospel. Their message utilized the Scriptures and declared the presence and power of sin. The good news of salvation in Christ was presented. The people were asked to make a decision.

THE PREACHING OF PAUL

Paul, the persecutor turned preacher, effectively communicated the gospel. We will examine two of his sermons. One was preached in a Jewish synagogue (Acts 13:16–41), the other in an outside meeting with philosophers and intellectuals (Acts 17:22–31). The approach of each message was appropriate to the audience, but both contained the same basic characteristics.

In the Jewish synagogue, Paul began with Israel's history (Acts 13:16–22). This approach probably produced understanding and appreciation from the group. Paul wanted to provide a historical link to Jesus, "From this man's [David] seed according to the promise, God raised up for Israel a Savior—Jesus" (v. 23). Paul recited several facts about Jesus: John's presentation (v. 25), death (vv. 27–29), and resurrection (vv. 30–37).

Paul clearly presented the offer of forgiveness from sins and a new relationship with God. He warned the people not to reject the offer. The message had a personal emphasis: "Therefore, my brothers, I want you to know that through Jesus the forgiveness of sins is proclaimed to you" (v. 38 NIV). Paul offered each person a personal invitation: "everyone who believes is justified" (v. 39). A decision needed to be made by each person.

Paul faced an entirely different audience in Athens. A group of philosophers and intellectual idol worshippers had listened with curious interest to Paul as "he preached to them Jesus and the resurrection" (Acts 17:18). Paul received an invitation to speak on the hill where the people of Athens and foreign visitors frequently discussed "some new thing" (v. 21). The message centered on God as the Creator, Guide, and Father who desires to have fellowship with all people. It was a new revelation to a people with gods of "gold or silver or stone" (v. 29). Repentance was asked of the philosophers and "all men everywhere" (v. 30). Paul warned them of the judgment day when the world will face Christ the resurrected Lord (v. 31).

Paul was more general in this message. He appealed to the mind so he could later speak to the heart. The type of challenge Stephen presented was inappropriate for this crowd who had never heard of Jesus and knew nothing of the Old Testament. Yet Paul preached the gospel and "some . . . believed" (v. 34). Paul had made them aware of sin and the need for repentance. He delivered the good news and some accepted.

Peter, Stephen, Philip, Paul—these were only a few of the first church leaders. Their sermons serve as examples and were probably typical of preaching done by others. These New Testament sermons share these similarities:

New Testament Sermons

1. Scripture was used and applied to life needs.
2. The message was good news about Jesus.
3. Sin was honestly faced.
4. The people were asked to obey God.

The preaching of Jesus provided the model for the disciple's preaching. The sermons you prepare should include these distinctives of New Testament preaching.

REACTION AND RESPONSE

For a perspective on Paul's message at Mars Hill, read Raymond Bailey, *Paul the Preacher* (Nashville: Broadman & Holman Publishers, 1991), 99–107.

Chapter 3
Why Preaching Today?

Effective biblical preaching comes from a preacher who is convinced preaching is essential. Why should there be preaching in our time? Many do not consider it necessary. There have always been people who deny the need for preaching. Paul said preaching is foolishness "to those who are perishing" (1 Cor. 1:18). Unfortunately, even some ministers have a low regard for preaching. A student preparing for the ministry said: "I consider preaching a necessary evil . . . I could well wish to avoid preaching almost entirely."[1] Other pastors give the preaching task too little of their time because they are convinced of its insignificance. Sometimes church members ask the pastor to do so many things he does not have enough time to adequately prepare for preaching. This may make the pastor feel preaching is not needed. Preachers who believe preaching is their most important assignment deliver the most effective sermons.

Every preacher should be committed to the importance of preaching. Keep uncertainty out of the pulpit. The Scripture gives at least four reasons for the necessity of preaching: (1) the opportunity for God to reveal Himself; (2) the example and command of Jesus; (3) the practice of the first Christians; (4) the need of people. May these reasons help strengthen your commitment to preaching.

THE OPPORTUNITY FOR GOD TO REVEAL HIMSELF

Clyde Fant wrote, "preaching continues . . . because it does what God did . . . to Israel . . . to the prophets and apostles . . . in Jesus."[2] God makes Himself known in a personal way. In preaching God continues to reveal Himself. Robert Mounce observes "that revelation and proclamation partake of the same nature. God reveals Himself in His acts, we said. And is not the redemptive activity of God in Christ Jesus the very heart of the *kerygma*? At this vital point, revelation and proclamation become one. Preaching is revelation."[3]

The second paragraph of the Bible begins, "Then God said" (Gen. 1:3). The last paragraph of the Bible closes with God saying: "Surely, I am coming soon" (Rev. 22:20). God reveals Himself through the spoken word. So through preaching God continues to reveal Himself.

The Old Testament chronicles God's work in the world using the Israelites to present His message to all people. Through the preaching of the prophets, the Lord made known His will. Notice these examples in Scripture of God revealing His will through the spoken word:

- Hear, O heavens! And give ear, O earth: For the Lord has spoken (Isa. 1:2).
- The word that came to Jeremiah from the Lord (Jer. 11:1).
- Jeremiah finished telling the people all the words of the Lord their God, everything the Lord has sent him to tell them (Jer. 43:1 NIV).
- The word of the Lord came to me (Ezek. 12:1).
- The Lord began to speak by Hosea (Hos. 1:2).
- The word of the Lord that came to Joel (Joel 1:1).
- Hear this word that the Lord has spoken against you, O children of Israel (Amos 3:1).
- Hear now what the Lord says (Mic. 6:1).
- The word of the Lord came by Haggai the prophet (Hag. 1:1).
- Again the word of the Lord of Hosts came saying (Zech. 8:1–2).

Biblical preaching differs from Old Testament prophecy, but both show that God reveals Himself through the spoken word. We preach today because God chooses to reveal Himself through the spoken word.

Words are inadequate. Has any young man ever possessed all the right words to tell his bride-to-be how much he loves her? God spoke, but it was not enough so "the Word became flesh and dwelt among us. We beheld His glory, the glory of the only begotten of the Father, full of grace and truth" (John 1:14). Jesus is God's message of love and forgiveness to the world. The book of Hebrews tells more about God's revelation:

> In the past God spoke to our forefathers through the prophets at many times and in various ways, but in these last days he has spoken to us by his Son, whom he appointed heir of all things. (Heb. 1:1–2 NIV)

The Lord revealed Himself to the prophets in the word. The full and complete Word from God is Jesus. When you preach Christ, God continues to speak to people. "Preaching is not talking about God; it is allowing God to talk."[4] In preaching God reveals Himself—"as though God were pleading through us" (2 Cor. 5:20).

THE EXAMPLE AND COMMAND OF JESUS

Jesus once said, "As the Father has sent me, I also send you" (John 20:21). What was His mission? He tells us, "I must preach the kingdom of God . . . because for this purpose I have been sent" (Luke 4:43). Jesus faithfully fulfilled His mission. "Jesus went about all Galilee . . . preaching the gospel of the kingdom" (Matt. 4:23). Jesus' example is reason enough why preaching continues today.

> All those who have trusted in God's only Son
> And hold this precious treasure in their hearts,
> Seek ways to make it known to all who need to know
> That God so loved the world his only Son he gave.[5]

There are many ways to make Christ known, including the Holy Ordinances and works of love, but we must follow the example of Jesus and give priority to preaching.

Preaching also continues because Jesus commanded it. Twelve were appointed "that they might be with him and that he might send them out to preach" (Mark 3:14). Jesus "gave them power and authority . . . he sent them to preach the kingdom of God" (Luke 9:1–2). That same commission has been given to the church. Christ commanded that "repentance and remission of sins should be preached in his name to all nations, beginning at Jerusalem. And you are witnesses of these things" (Luke 24:47–48). Peter said that Christ "commanded us to preach" (Acts 10:42). On an earlier occasion Peter was commanded by the authorities "not to speak at all nor teach in the name of Jesus" (Acts 4:18). However, he obeyed the command of Christ. Can a preacher today do less?

THE PRACTICE OF THE FIRST CHRISTIANS

To be a New Testament church, a body of believers should follow the practice of the New Testament. The first Christians emphasized preaching. Preaching the good news in a fellowship of faith and love resulted in daily additions to the church (Acts 2:47). The Lord blessed the efforts of these first

Christians. The enemies of Christ saw preaching as the primary tool of the church and tried to stop the preaching. They were "greatly disturbed that they taught the people and preached in Jesus the resurrection" (Acts 4:2). "Many of those who heard the word believed" and the Jerusalem Christians soon numbered five thousand men (Acts 4:4).

The church members prayed for their leaders to be bold preachers. "Now Lord . . . grant to your servants that with all boldness they may speak your word" (Acts 4:29).

The apostles led the church to select church helpers so the preachers would have more time to preach. Seven lay leaders were given responsibilities in the church so the apostles could give attention "to prayer and to the ministry of the word" (Acts 6:4). However, the deacons preached also! This sharing of work brought great results: "the word of God spread, and the number of disciples multiplied greatly" (Acts 6:7). When preaching the good news assumes a primary place in the church, the church will grow.

Persecution disrupted the worship services and congregational meetings in Jerusalem. Disciples scattered, but the primary work of the church continued. "Those who were scattered went everywhere preaching the word" (Acts 8:4). Preaching can be done anywhere and everywhere. Preaching needs no buildings nor budget. Churches often emphasize programs more than preaching the good news. The program of the first Christians was to proclaim the gospel. Strong churches today seek to follow the practice of the first Christians—they make preaching a priority.

THE NEED OF PEOPLE

A final reason why preaching continues in our time is the need of people. Paul wrote:

> Everyone who calls on the name of the Lord shall be saved. How, then, shall they call on him in whom they have not believed? And how shall they believe in him of whom they have not heard? And how shall they hear without a preacher? (Rom. 10:13–14)

> Preaching occupies a central place in the process of reaching the lost world. The Lord gives salvation, but individuals must trust Jesus Christ. They can not trust Him until they know about Him. Preaching tells people about Jesus and offers them the opportunity of salvation. "Faith comes by hearing, and hearing by the word of God." (Rom. 10:17)

God has chosen preaching as a primary means of giving His message of life to a dying world. The pastor must not put preaching at the bottom of his work in the church. The Lord desires to use your preaching to bring lost people to a saving knowledge of Jesus Christ. Preaching becomes urgent when the preacher realizes the lost are dying. A hymn expresses what every preacher should remember when delivering the good news.

> Brethren, see poor sinners round you
> Slumb'ring on the brink of woe;
> Death is coming, hell is moving
> Can you bear to let them go?[6]

Why does preaching continue to be done in our time? Scripture provides at least these four reasons: (1) the opportunity for God to reveal Himself; (2) the example and command of Jesus; (3) the practice of the first Christians; (4) the need of people. The Lord God reveals Himself in Christ to lost mankind as preachers proclaim the gospel. Jesus commanded us to preach and was the best example of how it should be done. The successful practice of preaching by the first Christians encourages every pastor and church to make preaching a priority today.

REACTION AND RESPONSE

Read Haddon W. Robinson "The Case for Expository Preaching," *Biblical Preaching* (Grand Rapids: Baker, 1980), 15–29.

Unit 2

Preparing the Preacher

What a risk the Lord takes to trust the proclamation of his inerrant Word to persons like us. Paul did not want to hinder the Word of God and requested his friends to pray for him "that the word of the Lord may run swiftly and be glorified" (2 Thess. 3:1). Since the message can be hindered by the preacher, an important part of sermon preparation is preparation of the preacher.

God prepares us in many ways. Life prepares us to preach. "We know that in all things God works for the good of those who love Him, who have been called according to His purpose" (Rom. 8:28 NIV). The Lord prepares us with life experiences of suffering and joy. George W. Truett, long-time pastor of Dallas First Baptist Church, accidentally shot and killed a member of his church on a hunting trip. Those who regularly heard him preach remarked about the noticable difference the experience made in his preaching. Afterwards, he seemed to speak with more empathy and urgency. The Lord encourages and prepares us through wise friends and stronger Christians. He prepares some by giving them waiting time, as Moses waited for years while God prepared him to lead Israel. God prepares his preachers through the many experiences of life.

Preachers are prepared in their personal encounter with the Lord. A growing life "in Christ" is the best preparation to preach. No preacher is ready to speak to others when he has not first listened to and talked with the Lord.

God prepares us to preach in the study. Sermon preparation is practical work. It involves the discipline of study. The Word of God must be interpreted and then communicated to the people in ways they will understand. When it comes to study, "the spirit indeed is willing, but the flesh is weak" (Matt. 26:41). Excuses are easily turned into reasons for not studying. But remember, effective biblical preaching requires much study.

God prepares those He calls to preach. The preparation of the preacher involves a lifelong process. The Lord's preparation depends on our cooperation. May Paul's commitment be ours, "I can do all things through Christ who strengthens me" (Phil. 4:13).

Chapter 4
Who Qualifies?

Each week the newspaper has job-opening advertisements which usually contain qualifications required for the needed employee. There are five qualifications required for those who want to be an effective preacher of God's Word. Some are stronger in one area than another. The most effective preachers possess all these qualifications.

KNOW THE LORD

God uses a born-again person to preach the good news of Christ. William Temple said, "Instead of saying 'Go to the cross,' we must be able to say 'Come to the cross.' And there are only two voices which can issue that invitation with effect. One is the voice of the Sinless Redeemer, with which we cannot speak; the other is the voice of the forgiven sinner, who knows himself forgiven. That is our part."[1]

The apostle John personally knew Jesus and could declare, "That which was from the beginning, which we have heard, which we have seen with our eyes, which we have looked upon, and our hands have handled concerning the Word of life" (1 John 1:1). Conversion reconciles the lost sinner to God in a personal encounter with Jesus Christ. Once reconciled, God gives us the "ministry of reconciliation" (2 Cor. 5:18).

On the Damascus Road, Paul was blinded by an encounter with Jesus. The Lord sent a man named Ananias with instructions for Paul's future. Ananias said to the new Christian, "You will be his witness to all men of what you have seen and heard" (Acts 22:15). Paul recalled Jesus' words to him on the day of his conversion, "I have appeared to you for this purpose, to make you a minister and a witness both of the things which you have seen and of the things which I will reveal to you" (Acts 26:16).

The strongest witness presented in a court comes from the eyewitness account of a trustworthy person. Preaching by a born-again individual is the word of an eyewitness. The missionary preacher E. Stanley Jones first trained to be a lawyer. When he began to preach, his first sermon was presented as a lawyer would give his side of the trial. Jones considered this first message a failure. Just before he left the room, he gave his testimony and a young man was saved. Jones later said, "That night marked a change in my conception of the work of the Christian minister—he is to be, not God's lawyer to argue well for God, but he is to be God's witness, to tell what grace has done for an unworthy life."[2] If you have any doubts about your conversion, talk with a trusted friend or pastor. Be able to say, "I know whom I have believed" (2 Tim. 1:12).

CALLED BY THE LORD

Have you had someone ask you, "When did God call you to preach?" The Bible has two meanings of the "call." God's call is general, to every Christian person. But it may also be specific. He calls individuals to leadership positions.

The Bible teaches that every person has been called by God. Those who respond in faith He justifies (Rom. 8:30). God calls every Christian to serve Him and to be His witness. Each believer is called to live a life of holiness (1 Thess. 4:7). "As he who called you is holy, you also be holy in all your conduct" (1 Pet. 1:15). Peter also said God has called us "out of darkness into his marvelous light" (1 Pet. 2:9). Every Christian shares the calling of God: "There is one body and one Spirit, just as you were called in one hope of your calling" (Eph. 4:4). According to 2 Cor. 5:18–20, each person made right with God becomes Christ's ambassador in the ministry of making others right with God. This general call gives every Christian the opportunity and obligation to preach the good news.

Another meaning of "call" in the Bible is more specific. God calls certain individuals to a lifework of preaching and leading churches. No one should make this his lifework unless God calls him. The certain knowledge of God's call keeps a preacher-pastor going when he may feel like quitting. Robert H. Mounce wrote, "Without this divine compulsion there can be no effective communication. While there may be an impartation of religious ideas, there will be no real preaching."[3]

Moses received God's call. "I will send you to Pharoah that you may bring my people, the children of Israel, out of Egypt" (Exod. 3:10). Moses protested because he could not understand why God would choose him. God never gave a reason for choosing Moses, but He did give him a tremendous promise. "I will certainly be with you" (Exod. 3:12).

God called a shepherd farmer named Amos. "The Lord God has spoken—who can but prophesy?" (Amos 3:8). Amos also expressed surprise that God would call and use a shepherd and farmer (Amos 7:14–15). God calls individuals with many different backgrounds and abilities. He knows the persons He can best use to preach the good news and lead the churches.

Isaiah experienced God's call in a time of national grief, "in the year that King Uzziah died" (Isa. 6:1). The land was going through change; leaders were needed. God asked, "Whom shall I send? And who will go for us?" Isaiah offered himself, and God responded, "Go, and tell this people" (Isa. 6:9). Maybe God caused you to see the need of our world and the lack of church leaders. You offered yourself. Did God call you and send you to the work?

God told Jeremiah he was chosen before birth! "Before you were born I sanctified you; I ordained you a prophet to the nations" (Jer. 1:5). Many called to be preachers have protested like Jeremiah that they could not speak. The person God calls also receives Jeremiah's promise, "I am with you to deliver you . . . Behold, I have put my words in your mouth" (Jer. 1:8–9).

The disciples were called (Mark 3:13–15). They were Christ's choice, "those He wanted." They served because "He appointed," and "that He might send them out to preach."

Paul wrote that God "separated me from my mother's womb and called me through His grace, to reveal his Son in me, that I might preach him" (Gal. 1:15–16). He felt compelled to preach. "Woe is me if I do not preach the gospel!" (1 Cor. 9:16). Severe persecution and many church problems never stopped Paul from preaching because God had called him.

My seminary professor and counselor, Dr. Clyde Francisco, once told me, "Did God call you to preach? Then preach; let nothing detract you from that central task." Although every Christian can preach, only those called by God should make preaching their lifework. God calls "some (to be) pastors and teachers, for the equipping of the saints for the work of ministry" (Eph. 4:11–12).

FOLLOW THE LORD

The Lord calls and sets apart the preacher to follow Christ as Lord of life, serve the church, and preach the Word. An effective preacher must be dedicated to the church, the Scripture, and to the Lord Jesus Christ. Paul's experience in Ephesus reveals these three dimensions of dedicated discipleship.

Paul was dedicated to the church. It is by the church that "the manifold wisdom of God might be made known . . . according to the eternal purpose which he accomplished in Christ Jesus our Lord" (Eph. 3:10–11). The Lord wants a preacher dedicated to building up the churches. Sermons that divide, antagonize, bruise the flock, and drive them away seem to violate this dimension of church dedication.

Acts 20:18–35 records Paul's farewell message to the Ephesian church leaders. It is an inspiring example of the preacher's love for the people of God, the church. The leaders are encouraged to "shepherd the church of God, which he purchased with His own blood" (v. 28). Paul expressed concern for the church's future (vv. 29–31) and its spiritual growth (v. 32). Paul and the leaders knelt together in prayer. "They all wept as they embraced him and kissed him" (v. 37 NIV). The scene shows the close relationship between Paul and the church he had served for three years. Following the Lord always includes loving relationship with God's people and building up the church.

Dedication to the Word of God is essential for God to use a preacher. Paul's ministry in Ephesus stressed God's Word. He preached that all Jews and Gentiles alike should have "repentance toward God and faith toward our Lord Jesus Christ" (Acts 20:21). "Preaching the kingdom" was his priority so he could say upon leaving the church, "I have not shunned to declare to you the whole counsel of God" (vv. 25–27).

The calling to preach is a calling to preach the inspired Word of God. God issues to every preacher the charge given to Timothy: "Preach the Word! Be ready in season and out of season. Convince, rebuke, exhort, with all longsuffering and teaching" (2 Tim. 4:2). The apostles refused to let secondary work destroy their devotion "to the ministry of the Word" (Acts 6:4).

Dedication to God's Word requires the preacher to study the Bible on a regular basis. C. H. Spurgeon wrote, "It is blessed to eat into the very soul of the Bible until at last . . . your spirit is flavoured with the words of the Lord . . . and the very essence of the Bible flows through you."[4]

The preacher's highest dedication belongs to the Lord Jesus Christ. We do not worship the church nor the Bible. Christ established the church and made possible the Scriptures. Christ is head of the church (Col. 1:18) and the central message to be preached (Col. 1:28). Paul resolved "not to know anything . . . except Jesus Christ and him crucified" (1 Cor. 2:2), so that "In all things He [Christ] may have the preeminence" (Col. 1:18).

At Ephesus Paul "served the Lord" (Acts 20:19). He faithfully labored even when warned about "prisons and hardships." "I consider my life worth nothing to me, if only I may finish the race and complete the task the Lord Jesus has given me—the task of testifying to the gospel of God's grace" (Acts 20:24 NIV). Christ should be the most important person in a preacher's life. Without that dedication, lesser persons, who may not have God's will as their commitment, become sources of primary influence. Do you follow Christ as Lord of your life?

God has set His preachers apart to follow the Lordship of Jesus. This involves dedication to love and serve the church and faithfully preach God's Word.

LIVE LIKE THE LORD

Christian character results from following Christ as Lord of your life. The fruit of the Spirit grows in the surrendered life (Gal. 5:16–24). This growth process faces hindrances because the Spirit and our sinful nature "are contrary to one another" (Gal. 5:17). You must be willing to grow and let the Holy Spirit produce the fruit of the Spirit. Daily decisions must be made to live the Christ-like life.

The Lord takes a great risk in using people who can sin to do His work. Paul compared us to "jars of clay" containing treasure. The clay jar can easily break; a preacher can sin. God still chooses to use us to demonstrate that "the power may be of God and not of us" (2 Cor. 4:7).

Scripture sets a high standard of conduct and character for a church leader (1 Tim. 3:1–7; 1 Pet. 5:1–4). Every relationship of life must be truly Christian, "above reproach." Any deed, word, or attitude which is unchristian can cause the preacher to "fall into reproach and in the snare of the devil" (1 Tim. 3:7).

An actor plays a part which is not really himself. The Greek word for actor is *hypokrites*, hypocrite. Some of Jesus' strongest words of warning and judgment were leveled against the hypocrites (Matt. 6:2–16; 23:13–27). The Word of God works in spite of being preached by a hypocrite, but frequently, when the truth becomes known about the unfaithful preacher, the fruit of his labor becomes discouraged, critical, or inactive. A preacher must be a person with genuine Christian character. Live like the Lord; practice what you preach!

FELLOWSHIP WITH THE LORD

A consistent devotional experience with Christ will deepen your life as a preacher and make you more useful. Jesus said, "He who abides in me and I in him, bears much fruit; for without me you can do nothing" (John 15:5). A daily time of prayer and personal Bible study helps fulfill this need. E. M.

Bounds stated, "Preaching is not the performance of an hour. It is the outflow of a life." John R. W. Stott wrote, "The preparation of the heart is of far greater importance than the preparation of the sermon."[5]

You are not ready to preach until you have prayed, so prepare yourself through prayer. The apostles gave themselves to prayer (Acts 6:4). Without prayer, preaching becomes simply religious talk. The Jerusalem church prayed, and "they were all filled with the Holy Spirit, and they spoke the word of God with boldness" (Acts 4:31). Fervent prayer and spiritual communion with the Lord puts the preacher in touch with God's power. Responsible for one or two messages a week, a preacher frequently studies the Bible only for preaching. Personal prayer and devotional Bible study of the word for his own needs are overlooked. Soon the preaching loses its power, missing the strength which comes from a daily personal encounter with Christ.

A store clerk described the Scottish preacher Peter Marshall. "He seems to know God, and he helps me to know Him better."[6] When Moses came down from the mountain, his face reflected God's glory. Preaching should reflect the glory of God discovered in the preacher's personal communion with Christ.

Five qualifications of an effective preacher have been examined. The preacher should (1) know the Lord, (2) accept His call, (3) follow Christ the Lord in faithfully serving the church and preaching the Bible, (4) live the Christ-like life, and (5) nurture a consistent personal fellowship with the Lord.

REACTION AND RESPONSE

Study Stephen F. Olford, "The Walk to Pursue," *Annointed Expository Preaching* (Nashville: Broadman & Holman Publishers, 1998), 7–65.

Chapter 5
The Preacher's Authority

Religious leaders once questioned Jesus, "By what authority are you doing these things? Who gave you this authority?" (Matt. 21:23). These same questions may be asked of you. Where does a preacher secure his authority to preach? Local governments issue a license to perform marriages, and some churches grant a "license to preach," but this is not the source of the preacher's authority. Authority to preach comes from God. This lesson looks at three ways God gives authority to preach.

The Bible teaches that God has all authority and is the source of all authority. "There is no authority except from God" (Rom. 13:1). Even Satan's evil earthly uses of authority are permitted by God for a season (Luke 4:6). At the end of time all "authority and power" will be destroyed (1 Cor. 15:24).

Christ, God in human flesh, possessed eternal authority. The evidence was seen in His work. "The people were astonished at His teaching, for he taught them as one having authority" (Matt. 7:29). Jesus commanded "even the unclean spirits," and they obeyed Him (Mark 1:27). Jesus claimed "authority over all flesh" (John 17:2). The Lord now rules in heaven with "angels and authorities and powers . . . subject to Him" (1 Pet. 3:22). God has all authority, and Jesus, the God-man, displayed that authority.

Jesus' wilderness temptation offers a case study on dealing with power and authority. Satan tempted Jesus "to substitute power for authority." If Jesus would turn the stones to bread, the people would follow. Jesus also refused to gain authority "by compromise with existing powers." He would not bow down to Satan nor bless the status quo. Neither would the Lord throw Himself from the temple. As Raymond Bailey noted, "Jesus repudiated authority based on magic, compromise, or spectacle."[1]

Any authority a preacher now has is given by God and should be received as a trust from Christ. The preacher's position as Christ's steward carries authority. The message proclaimed adds authority.

AUTHORITY—A TRUST FROM CHRIST

In Mark 13:34, Jesus is likened to a home owner away on a journey. The servants are left "in charge, each with his assigned task (NIV)." "Charge" is the Greek word for authority. Until Jesus comes again, we who work in the church are "in charge, each with his assigned task." Preachers have authority from Christ to proclaim the gospel. That is their work until Jesus comes. The preacher represents Christ and must never replace Him. The ultimate authority resides in Christ's hands. The servants will give an account to the Home Owner when He returns.

The twelve disciples were called by Jesus and He "gave them power and authority" (Luke 9:1). They went out to preach upon His authority. A similar commission was issued just before Christ's bodily return to heaven: "And Jesus came and spoke to them, 'All authority has been given to me in heaven and on earth has been given to me. Go therefore [because of His authority] and make disciples of all the nations'" (Matt. 28:18–19).

Paul thought of himself as a steward. A steward was "the manager of a household . . . to whom the head of a house entrusted the management of his affairs. Steward is a descriptive title for all who have the privilege of preaching God's word, particularly in the ministry."[2] Paul uses this word in his letter to Corinth. "Let a man so consider us as servants of Christ and stewards of the mysteries of God. Moreover now it is required that in stewards that one be found faithful" (1 Cor. 4:1–2). This pattern for Christian ministry was needed in the Corinthian church. Leadership divided the congregation. Three of the leaders were gifted and powerful preachers (1 Cor. 1:10–12), but the church was reminded that each of these preachers had a trust from Christ. Authority must not be fought over but respected and used for the glory of Christ and the good of the church. Each worker will one day face the head of the church and be judged (1 Cor. 3:10–15). As a steward, the preacher should faithfully use the authority entrusted to him by Christ.

AUTHORITY—THE POSITION PLACED BY CHRIST

The steward had certain authority because of the position he was given by the master of the house. Other servants did not have his position nor his

The Preacher's Authority

responsibility. When responsibility is given, authority is necessary to do the job. If an individual is given responsibility to drive a truckload of merchandise to market, he has the authority to use the truck. However, it would be irresponsible, after he has unloaded the truck, to rent it out to someone else and make money on the side. A pastor-preacher placed in a leadership position has authority to do the job. Paul reminded the Corinthians of his authority in the church. "For even if I should boast about our authority which the Lord gave us for edification and not for destruction" (2 Cor. 10:8).

A pastor "is entrusted with God's work" (Titus 1:7 NIV). This phrase "entrusted with" translates the Greek word "steward." With the trust comes the authority to pastor, teach, and lead the church. How is this authority to be used? The pastor must not be "self-willed, not quick-tempered . . . not violent . . . but . . . self-controlled" (Titus 1:7–8). Peter gave this guideline for the use of authority by church leaders:

> Shepherd the flock of God which is among you, serving as overseers, not by compulsion but willingly, not for dishonest gain but eagerly; nor as being lords over those entrusted to you, but being examples to the flock; and when the Chief Shepherd appears, you will receive the crown of glory that does not fade away. (1 Pet. 5:2–4)

Does this describe a dictator-leader? A shepherd has authority but uses it in love. When God places a leader over a group, the leader is not their master. Christ is the only Lord.

The disciples once argued about the position of greatness in their group. Jesus said to them, "the kings of the Gentiles exercise lordship over them; and those who exercise authority over them are called benefactors. But not so among you, on the contrary, he who is greatest among you, let him be as the younger, and he who governs as he who serves" (Luke 22:24–26).

Hebrews 13:17 recognizes the authority of church leaders. Christians are told to "obey your leaders and submit to their authority. They keep watch over you as men who must give an account. Obey them so that their work will be a joy, not a burden, for that would be no advantage to you" (NIV). People follow a leader who leads like Christ. A pastor-preacher must earn the respect and loyalty of the people he serves. Good relationships must be developed. The pastor and the people must know each other. When the pastor proves trustworthy, the people will trust him more. When the pastor abuses authority, the people have the right to look to Jesus for another leader. Leadership of the church must find confirmation by the church. One can't lead those who are unwilling to follow or trust the leader. The wisdom of the body provides a corrective to the pastor's excesses.

Two sources of authority have been noted. Authority is a trust given by Christ who called you into the ministry. Authority is in the position of responsibility where the Lord places you to serve. Authority also abides in the message Christ gives you to preach.

AUTHORITY—THE MESSAGE CHRIST GIVES

Jesus was the Word, the truth. As such He could say, "Truly, truly, I say unto you." All authority was in Him. A preacher today does not have that total authority. Our spoken word will be tested by the standard of Scripture. We have the authority of God's Word. Evangelist Billy Graham shows a "sense of authority" when he preaches. In his messages he will often say, "The Bible says." As Clyde Fant wrote, "He is convinced that the message does not originate with him, nor is the power and authority his. Therefore, he is able to speak with confidence and yet with humility."[3]

The young preacher Timothy was told to "give attention" to Scripture and preaching (1 Tim. 4:13). He was to "turn away from godless chatter and the opposing ideas of what is falsely called knowledge" (1 Tim. 6:20 NIV). His life was to be immersed in the Holy Scriptures. He was encouraged to become familiar with all the Scripture "so that the man of God may be complete, thoroughly equipped for every good work" (2 Tim. 3:14–17). If you follow Timothy's example, your preaching will have authority.

Christ sent Paul "to preach the gospel—not with wisdom of words, lest the cross of Christ should be made of no effect" (1 Cor. 1:17). Power and authority go together. To preach anything other than the gospel is to lose God's power and authority.

> And I, brethren, when I came to you, did not come with excellence of speech or of wisdom declaring to you the testimony of God. For I determined not to know anything among you except Jesus Christ and Him crucified. I was with you in weakness, in fear, and in much trembling. And my speech and my preaching were not with persuasive words of human wisdom, but in demonstration of the Spirit and of power. (1 Cor. 2:1–5)

Albert Mohler Jr. wrote, "The issue of authority is inescapable. Either the preacher or the text will be the operant authority. A theology of preaching serves to remind those who preach of the danger of confusing our own authority with that of the biblical text. We are called, not only to *preach*, but to preach *the Word*."[4]

The Preacher's Authority

A government sends an ambassador with a message. He has no authority to speak his own ideas or message. The steward is asked to manage the houseowner's affairs. He must use his energies to direct what is another's and not destroy it. The steward has authority to do what the master instructs. The preacher has authority to preach the Word; anything less becomes unfaithfulness. Anything more becomes irresponsibility.

In summary, the preacher's authority derives from three sources. It is a trust from Christ who has all authority and calls the preacher into the ministry. Authority rests in the position of leadership where Christ, acting through His church, places you to serve. Authority also abides in the Word of God. In each of these areas of authority, the preacher must be a faithful steward and use his authority for the good of the church. The preacher must serve under the Lordship of Christ before whom all preachers will one day stand to be judged.

REACTION AND RESPONSE

Relate this lesson to the four sources of the preacher's authority found in George Sweazey, *Preaching the Good News* (N. J.: Prentice Hall, 1976), 25–31.

Chapter 6
Excuses for Inadequate Preparation

Worthy goals should motivate our ministry. Adopt the goal of doing your best in sermon preparation. Through God's grace, this book will help you achieve that goal. Whenever God's servants attempt their best, Satan works against them. He will provide excuses to make us feel better when we have not done our best. Instead of making excuses, choose the best solution: repentance and a new direction with Christ's help.

You will grow in your preaching ability as you resist the excuses listed below. Find ways to turn these problems into helps for your ministry. You will probably use these excuses and others. Not one of these excuses is a satisfactory reason for you to to deliver a poorly prepared message.

EXCUSE NUMBER ONE:
I DO NOT HAVE THE TIME

Suppose someone gave you $86,400 each day with only one requirement—you must use all of it or lose what is left. WOW! Right now I can think of many needed things and a few wants. Nothing would be left at the end of the first few days. Yet, you have been given something more valuable than money. Eighty-six thousand, four hundred seconds are yours to use each day. The time you do not use, you will lose. Each of us has the same amount of time, and we must make decisions about how we use it. If God has called you to preach, you will find time to study and prepare. Since you must prepare for preaching, you will not be able to use your time as those who do not preach. Make sermon preparation your first business, and you will always have time for preparation.

A preacher lives and works in a world of time. The Bible says, "There is a time for everything" (Ecc. 3:1). Do you preach at least once a week? Every week you know that time is coming. The moment you finish preaching the sermon for this week, you know another sermon must be done next week. The time is set. Prepare for it!

Consider this suggestion which might be helpful for the better use of your time. At the start of each day (or the night before) make a list of things you must do. Rank the items according to which is most important. After your prayer and Bible study time, start to work on the first item on your list. If your day runs out before your list, place as No. 1 for the next day the item which was next. You will accomplish more with your time if you plan how to use it. If you do not plan, others will set plans for you. Don't forget, in the above plan, to place sermon preparation as a priority.

Be prepared for interruptions. Someone will come by to talk when you need to study. Listen to see if there is a problem; God may have sent the person so you could help. But if he or she just wants to visit, you will soon have to say, "Friend, I'm glad you came. I will talk with you later. Now, I must prepare my sermon for Sunday."

Do not put off your responsibilities. Start early. You may surprise yourself and finish ahead of schedule and have time for something else. Early preparation produces a stronger sermon. Thoughts and ideas will have time to settle and mix. Illustrations will be noticed. You will have time to rearrange the message and prepare it in a better way when you start early. Later chapters in this text will consider sermon planning and preliminary study.

Make use of time that is sometimes "lost" doing nothing or while waiting for an appointment. Use the time by taking along something to read. Observe people and events as you travel; you will see many sermon illustrations. Listen and share your witness with people around you. We have much to learn from others. Are you "redeeming the time, because the days are evil?" (Eph. 5:16). Could your leisure time be shortened? Are you watching too much television or too many home videos?

Those who work in a secular job and also preach regularly have more pressure on them regarding time. Look for a period of time throughout the day when you might get in some extra moments of study. The working day is full of ideas and illustrations. Keep your eyes open and a notepad handy on which to write "flashes of inspiration" as they come. They will later be the source of sermons.

"I do not have the time" is no reason for poor sermon preparation. You must learn to use your time effectively and make sermon preparation a priority in the time available. Jeffrey Mayer offers excellent suggestions for time management in his interesting book, *If You Haven't Got the Time to Do It Right, When Will You Find the Time to Do It Over?*[1]

EXCUSE NUMBER TWO:
I HAVE FAMILY RESPONSIBILITIES

Family responsibilities may prevent a preacher from preparing his sermons. Sometimes a child or another member of the family may be ill, and he will lose sleep or be at the hospital helping to care for the ill person. A preacher should not neglect his family. "If anyone does not provide for his own, and especially for those of his household, he has denied the faith and is worse than an unbeliever" (1 Tim. 5:8).

Paul warned about family pressures in the ministry. "But he who is married cares about the things of the world, how he may please his wife . . . And this I say for your own profit, not that I may put a leash on you, but for what is proper, and that you may serve the Lord without distraction" (1 Cor. 7:33–35). A preacher needs a spouse who will support his ministry. She should understand and share his devotion to Christ and preaching. She will then help him use his time to prepare. He will plan to use some of his best time to share with her and the family.

Parents are part of your responsibility. You are to "honor your father and your mother" (Exod. 20:12). If they are Christians, they will likely encourage you to be the best preacher you can be. If your parents are not Christians, you will need extra grace and strength to honor them without dishonoring Christ.

Jesus had family pressures. Mary and her other children did not at first support Jesus in His ministry. His family "went out to lay hold of him, for they said, 'He is out of his mind.'" When they asked to see Jesus, He responded, "Who is my mother, or my brothers? . . . For whoever does the will of God is my brother and and my sister and mother" (Mark. 3:20–21, 33–35). Jesus placed God's will as His highest priority. God's will involves the best for your family. Jesus' loving attitude and care for Mary, displayed at the cross, illustrate how God's will and family responsibility go together.

Family relationships never kept Jesus from doing God's will. "He who loves father or mother more than me is not worthy of me; And he who loves son or daughter more than me is not worthy of me; and he who does not take his cross and follow after me is not worthy of me" (Matt. 10:37–38). Family responsibilities must not be an excuse for lack of sermon preparation and faithful ministry.

EXCUSE NUMBER THREE:
THE CHURCH REQUIRES TOO MUCH

Most preachers serve as pastors. The church members expect the pastor to do certain things. The pastor's role includes many jobs: counseling, administration, relationships with other churches, mission outreach, recreation, community affairs, teaching, and preaching. Each church member has ideas about which part of the pastor's job is the most important. Preaching is not a priority for every church member, and you will feel pressure from the church to devote more time to less important things.

Try to solve this problem before you accept a pastorate. Talk with the church and its leaders. How important is preaching to them? Stress the importance of your call to preach. Will they support you in this? Will they honor your study time? God may want you to serve as their pastor even if you disagree. You will then have the opportunity to lead them to a better understanding and appreciation of preaching.

Some church work is good and needed. What a particular church expects may be the result of the members seeking and finding God's will for their church. An effective leader will not fight against this. Instead, he will develop leaders who can take some of the responsibility, as the Jerusalem church did with the seven chosen to distribute food to the widows.

A pastor-preacher needs to use his role as an equipper of church members. God gave the church "some pastors and teachers, for the equipping of the saints for the work of ministry, for the edifying of the body of Christ" (Eph. 4:11–12). God never asks a pastor to do all the work of the church. Your position involves training and teaching others to share the work of ministry.

Are you willing to share responsibility in the church? Are you secure in your position as pastor-leader? Are you afraid someone will try to "take over"? Do you get jealous if someone else gets attention or is recognized for a job well-done in the church? These questions must be honestly faced. Some pastors use the excuse, "The church expects me to do too much," when the problem is a failure to train someone else or to delegate the responsibility to another. Others could do it just as well as you can. Letting others do some church tasks will free you for the priority of preaching and also provide quality time for your family.

EXCUSE NUMBER FOUR: I DID NOT STUDY ENOUGH

This is a fourth excuse preachers use to justify poor sermon preparation. Is it a lack of faith to study? Some answer with a quote from Jesus, "Do not worry about how or what you should speak. For it will be given to you in that hour what you should speak" (Matt. 10:19). Jesus was not talking about preaching, but the testimony given in a time of persecution. A preacher must face this command: "Be diligent to present yourself approved to God, a worker who does not need to be ashamed, rightly dividing the word of truth" (2 Tim. 2:15). Without study, a preacher has not done his best. Study is work!

It is one way the preacher has of preparing himself for presenting the gospel. Study helps the preacher "rightly divide the word." Without study, the Scripture may be incorrectly interpreted or applied in the wrong way. The Holy Spirit leads in the study time as well as in the pulpit. Make every effort to study before your preach. You will then not have to use the excuse, "I did not study enough."

Adequate study results from regular study habits. A regular time and place for study encourages better preparation. Determine the best time for you to study. Some preachers are "night people" and have fewer interruptions during late hours. Whatever time is best, keep faith with it. Relationships with church members and better support from them would improve if the people know your usual time for study

A study plan will be helpful. Of course, you will study for the next message you are to preach. Your study time should also include work for preaching needs of the future. Study through a book of the Bible. A topic can be examined—what does the Bible say about death, greed, or another topic? Study problems your people are facing: violence, marriage, financial stress. Read a variety of materials such as a news magazine, a theological journal, a biography, a novel, or current books of interest to your people. Wide reading will generate ideas, illustrations, and keep you informed.

Books are expensive, and you may never have all you want, but set a goal to save and purchase books which will strengthen your ministry. Buy used books and watch for discounts. Develop your library by purchasing one good commentary set and then purchase books on individual books of the Bible or subject areas on which you are preaching. Over a period of time your library will have more diversity. Read at a school or public library. Everyday events, the world of science and nature, the stories of famous and not so famous people will make your preaching more interesting.

Study will produce much information. Take notes as you read and study. Work out a system to keep these notes and know where the information is when you need it. A later chapter will focus on some methods for storing materials and making the most of preparation time.

There will be times, even after you have studied several hours on a sermon, that you will feel you need to study more. However, you will have to preach. The time has run out even with your planning and preparation. In that case you will not use the excuse, "I did not study enough." You did study. Maybe you will have an opportunity to preach the message again and can make it stronger for that occasion. This excuse applies to the preacher who has had the time to study and did not use it. Every week there is time to study. You must make sermon preparation a priority.

There are many other excuses used to justify inadequate sermon preparation We have considered four: *I do not have enough time. I have family responsibilities. The church requires too much. I did not study enough.* Did you notice that each excuse relates to a positive area of your life? Time, family, church, and study are all needed for effective preaching. Paul wrote, "Do not let your good be spoken of as evil" (Rom. 14:16). Commitment and discipline in your life will turn these excuses into excellent resources.

REACTION AND RESPONSE

If you are a pastor, what work are you now doing in the church that could be done by someone else? Who could be trained for this or is already able to assume this responsibility?

Do a two-week time study. Keep a chart of how you use your time. What changes should you make?

Unit 3

Understanding the Word

Units 3 through 5 take a closer look at each of the basic steps in sermon preparation. These rest upon a daily fellowship with Christ and the leadership of the Holy Spirit.

- Choose and interpret a text.
- Decide on objectives.
- Prepare a thesis sentence and title.
- Develop the body of the sermon.
- Prepare the conclusion and invitation.
- Prepare the introduction.

The most important part of this process is choosing the sermon text and determining the correct interpretation. It is possible to step lightly over this and prepare a message, but it will not be biblical. Preaching is the proclamation of the good news of Jesus. The will of God is made known through the Scriptures inspired by the Holy Spirit. In the next lessons you will study principles for finding a text and interpreting it. A building must have an adequate foundation to support the superstructure. Prayer and text interpretation require work. Resist the temptation to treat this with less importance. What happens to a building with an inadequate foundation?

"If I can find a better sermon, I'll preach it!" some preachers joke. Although for some, maybe more than I realize, it isn't a joke. Not long after formal training has been completed, with the push of members' expectations, a preacher hungrily looks upon the published sermons of "successful preachers." A new meaning of "justified" enters the practice of his life, and soon the easy road becomes paved with someone else's work. The exhilarating fulfillment of discovering truth mined by personal study goes the way of expediency. A long time ago the realization dawned upon me that I was not gifted like others. I gratefully accepted my calling and gifts and determined to use them. Jesus said He would "make me to become." He can't make any of us what He desires when we keep offering to Him what someone else has done. Maybe that's part of the reason David refused Saul's armor. David did what he could do, and the Lord did the rest!

Chapter 7
Where Does He Find Those Great Ideas?

Taking out the trash from our house usually falls to me. We live on a campus with trash and garbage pickup at designated places, and our house isn't one of those. So the garbage bag goes in the trunk to be thrown out when I go to work. It doesn't take much sometimes to get my mind on the concerns of the day, and the trash remains in the trunk. My wife and I took a trip to Asheville, North Carolina, and stopped to shop. When I opened the trunk to put in a package, we found two bags of trash. Maybe that odor wasn't all coming from the paper mill down the road! I've got this idea for a sermon with a possible title, "Throwing Away the Trash," based on Philippians 3:1–10. Paul made the radical decisions to count as rubbish some very treasured possessions. How do we determine what to trash? Will we throw it away, or get busy and forget it? The idea may become just an opening illustration to what is a far more important issue. You check it out. Sermon ideas do come in unexpected ways. Be careful; some good ones may be thrown out in the trash.

Getting started is often the hardest part of sermon preparation. When Moses was sent to be God's spokesman he asked, "What shall I say to them?" (Exod. 3:13). Begin like Moses and ask God what to preach! Pray for sermon ideas and texts to preach. In the concordance, "preach" immediately follows "prayer." Biblical preaching begins with prayer. Jeremiah, uncertain about his preaching, was told to say "whatever I command you" (Jer. 1:7–9). Jeremiah preached, trusting God to give him the message.

Paul requested the Ephesians to pray that "whenever I open my mouth, words may be given me so that I will fearlessly make known the mystery of the gospel" (Eph. 6:19 NIV). Paul expected God to give him the words to say.

God gives the message in the study and in the pulpit. Inspiration comes when we study, pray, and observe God's world.

A sermon begins with an idea, the basic thought of the message. What is the sermon all about? As you face the next preaching responsibility, first ask God for an idea. Trust Him to provide you, His representative, the message He desires to be preached.

God may use the observations of church members, readings, conversations we have, and Bible study to impress upon you an idea. The realization that this is what God wants you to say will excite you about the message. You will be encouraged to prepare.

A SUITABLE IDEA

Not all ideas will be suitable for developing a sermon. Ask these three questions about your possible ideas. Is it biblical? Does it relate to life needs? Is it adequate?

Is the idea biblical? The idea must be supported by the Scripture. Community organizations or political groups may try to influence you to speak about programs or ideas they support. The advice to Timothy applies to you. "Avoiding the profane and idle babble and contradictions of what is falsely called knowledge—by professing it some have strayed concerning the faith" (1 Tim. 6:20–21). Every idea must be biblical. God would never give you an idea that has no support in the Bible. A specific text may not on occasions fit exactly your message, but the idea must be supported by Scripture truths and specific Bible references.

A friend of mine told me about the church he attended as a youth. "The pastor's sermons were more about world affairs, such as the United Nations, and he did not preach the Bible." The friend eventually found a church where biblical sermons were preached. Social and ethical issues are a source of many ideas, but these ideas must be supported by the Bible. A close relationship between the idea and a Scripture passage will produce a stronger sermon.

Does the idea relate to life needs? The Lord sends us to meet the needs of people. We preach to people. Ask God to give you ideas that meet people's needs. Genesis 6 records information about Noah and the ark. While reading this passage, one might become interested in the detail of the ark's construction. A carpenter would find this interesting, but, as an idea for a sermon, it does not relate enough to life needs. As we shall later note, neither should the passage be interpreted allegorically.

Passages in Revelation contain descriptions of beasts and other creatures. Preachers have used these to interpret the last days. The message may be interesting but without any relation to life. A suitable idea relates to life needs.

Is the idea adequate? Your sermon idea should contain enough truth for a complete message. It might make a good illustration for one part of a message, but can you build an entire sermon on it?

A sports-minded person in the church may request you to preach a sermon on the idea, "Our church must have a basketball team." This is neither an adequate nor biblical idea. The issue of a church basketball team should be decided by the church. If and when the church decides to form a team, then you could preach a sermon using the text 1 Cor. 9:22: "I have become all things to all men, that I might by all means save some." This consecrative sermon would seek to get the members to dedicate themselves to winning people for Christ. A basketball team becomes one "possible means" of reaching people. The original idea was inadequate for a sermon, although it does provide an illustration for a stronger biblical idea.

A suitable sermon idea will meet these three requirements: it will be biblical, adequate, and relevant to life. As you follow the Lord's will, pray and maintain regular study habits, He will give you ideas to preach. An idea should really excite you and motivate you to develop it for the people. Each sermon idea must have the assurance of having come from the Lord.

WHERE CAN I GET GOOD IDEAS?

The Lord will use many sources to produce ideas for your sermons. As a preacher of biblical sermons, the most important source of sermon ideas is the Bible. A daily Bible study time produces sermon ideas. The Bible contains an endless source of material related to life needs and problems. The emotions of hate, love, jealousy, fear, grief, gratitude, joy, and anger are all described in the Bible. The experiences of Bible persons are similar to present day experiences. Picture yourself in the biblical event. Think about how you would feel and act. The Scriptures give guidance for our relationships with family, work, government, church, friends, and enemies. Cultivate the Bible as your best source of sermon ideas.

I strongly recommend seeking the Lord's direction on preaching through books or sections of the Bible. These series of messages could be interspersed with sermons on seasonal themes, church needs, or doctrinal themes. Preaching through the Bible testifies to a preacher's walk by faith. You trust the Lord to give you a message from the next block of material. Each section of

Scripture will contain at least one preaching idea. Some preachers take a one week or longer study break each summer to seek the Lord's direction for the book(s) of the Bible they should preach on the following year. I shall never forget my experience in preaching through Numbers. Almost every week, something in the text related to needs in the church, community, or nation. The personalities of the book always found common ground with the people to whom I preached. A written version of the series was later accepted by a national preaching magazine.

The use of a lectionary offers another approach to systematic preaching of the entire Bible. A lectionary covers all the main teachings of the Scriptures in a three-year period. One pastor described the lectionary, "as a beginning place when I'm without strong direction for a Sunday text. I find myself using it about one-third of the time. The lectionary makes me consider Scripture passages that I often neglect."

Neglecting some sections of the Bible will cause you to overlook many suitable ideas. All Scripture is inspired and useful. Several years ago I listed the sermons I had preached at our church during the previous three years. The list was grouped by books of the Bible. To my surprise I discovered I had not preached a sermon from about fifteen books of the Bible. Read and study from all the Bible, and your source of ideas will be expanded.

New ideas often come by reading different translations. Compare these two readings of Acts 21:13–14:

> Then Paul answered, What mean ye to weep and to break mine heart? For I am ready not to be bound only, but also to die at Jerusalem for the name of the Lord Jesus. And when he would not be persuaded, we ceased, saying, The will of the Lord be done. (KJV)

> Why all this hysteria? Why do you insist on making a scene and making it even harder on me? You're looking at this backwards. The issue in Jerusalem is not what they do to me, whether arrest or murder, but what the Master Jesus does through my obedience. Can't you see that? (Eugene Peterson, *The Message*)

During my daily Bible reading, Peterson's contemporary translation spoke to me in a fresh new way. The passage continued to generate ideas in my mind about our relationship to God and how Paul kept his commitment to do the will of God. I later noted an outline for a sermon which I later preached.

What Is the Issue? Acts 21:1–14

I. Have you let a physical limitation become the issue? Paul refused to let a thorn in the flesh keep him from doing God's will. (2 Cor. 12.7)

II. Have you let position become the issue? (Phil. 3.4–11)
III. Have you let possessions become the issue? (Phil. 4: 11–13,19)

What is the issue for you? Can you say, "The issue is not what happens to me, but what the Master Jesus does through my obedience."

One year our church observed a "Read through The Bible" emphasis. Each week the people were asked to read a portion of Scripture, so that in a year all the Bible would be read. I decided to preach a sermon from the Scriptures they had read the previous week. When I trusted the Lord to give me a message from the designated passages, He always did. As a result I preached from all the Bible. Most of the weekly sections contained several ideas which were later developed and preached. My pulpit approach encouraged the people to keep their commitment and generated higher interest.

Every preacher lives in the midst of sermon ideas. Life experiences are filled with these ideas waiting to be developed. Do you see them? Are you listening? The preaching of Jesus offers the best example of this. He saw a freshly painted burial vault and preached about hypocrisy (Matt. 23:27). The flowers of the field and the birds of the air were the idea for teachings on anxiety (Matt. 6:25–30). Children playing in the marketplace gave Jesus a truth on selfish faultfinding people (Luke 7:31–35). Train your eyes and ears to notice sermon ideas.

While waiting for my wife to come from the grocery store, a man asked me to move my car so he could leave, explaining "I can only go forward; it won't go into reverse." I thought it would be wonderful if our churches didn't have any reverse gear and only went forward. The experience will be used to illustrate or provide the nucleus for a sermon on the church which Christ has called "Forward through the Ages."

Your own life experiences provide abundant ideas. One day our daughter Mary (then only three years old) asked me, "Daddy, how do you spell love?" Her question became the title and opening illustration for a Father's Day sermon. The way our Lord helped me to overcome a time of depression became a message entitled, "Staying on the Road of Joy and Gladness." Don't be hesitant to use your own experiences. People will appreciate your sincerity and the message will carry the authority of personal experience.

The experiences of others also provide sermon ideas. Be very careful not to embarrass individuals from the pulpit or tell something they do not desire told.

Throughout the year special events and holidays stimulate sermon ideas. Many people are thinking about the special day; why not follow their interest and preach a message on the idea? In 1985, the Philippines had a major emphasis on Mary which was to be launched on Sunday, September 8. In Manila, where

I pastored, banners and posters about Mary were everywhere. That Sunday morning I preached a sermon on the subject, "Mary, Mother of Jesus." Of course, the sermon was of major interest to the predominantly Catholic audience. Maybe you can develop some sermons from these special day ideas:

Special Event	Sermon Title	Text
New Year	You Have Not Passed This Way Before	Josh. 3:1–4
Valentine's Day	A Valentine from the Heart of God	1 John 3:1–3
Easter	The Dark Day Called Good Friday	Luke 23:44–54
Mother's Day	A Praiseworthy Mother	Prov. 31:10–31
Father's Day	Walking in Dad's Footsteps	1 Kings 22:41–53
Independence Day	Are You Free?	John 8:31–37
Memorial Day	Death Offers More Than Memory	2 Cor. 5:6–11
Christmas	Born to Make Us Family	Gal. 4:4–5

A wide variety of reading generates ideas. In chapter 6, you were encouraged to include reading in your study time. Reading from newspapers, novels, and magazines will introduce you to many ideas for possible sermons. Radio and television have much influence on people. Ideas gained from these sources will frequently be recognized by people at church. Many have also heard the commercials, seen the programs, or know the star. This creates more interest in your sermon.

PLAN AHEAD

A preacher asks for problems when he waits until late in the week to get an idea and work on a message. I've had my share of so-called "Saturday night miracles" which I have since thrown out of my file. Plan ahead. Always carry a note pad with you on which you can write down ideas as they come to you. Other things may cause you to forget the idea if you do not write it down. Some preachers maintain an "Idea Folder" into which they place ideas gleaned from reading and observation.

Chapter 23 will offer suggestions for planning your preaching. You can utilize folders designated for each week of the year or arranged by seasonal concerns. After considering the needs of the church, plan what you will preach each Sunday. List these ideas with possible texts. As you read, study, and serve people, additional ideas, illustrations, and supporting material for these proposed sermons will come to you. Record and place these materials in the appropriate folder. With many different ideas, sermon preparation is easier.

LET THE IDEA MATURE

Fruit must mature before it can be eaten. Most sermon ideas need time to mature before they can be fully developed into a sermon. The farmer sows the seed and waits for the final harvest. Many things happen before the harvest: rain, sunlight, and work by the farmer. A sermon idea also needs some help to make it more productive. Relate the idea to your own experience. Try to remember past experiences which may illustrate the idea. Think about those to whom you will preach the message. How will they receive the idea? Use your imagination. Write the idea in different words. Ask someone what they think about the idea. After you have done some study on the idea, leave it for a while. Later you will probably have some other thoughts and material which will be remembered. Mature your sermon idea and use it at the right time.

Let's review the content of this chapter. A sermon begins with an idea given to you by God as a result of earnest prayer. This sermon idea, the basic thought of the message, must be suitable for a biblical sermon and meet the test of these three concerns: Is the idea biblical? Does the idea relate to life needs? Is the idea adequate?

God uses many sources to give you ideas to preach. The most important source is the Bible. A regular Bible study time will produce more ideas than you will likely use. Other sermon idea sources are life experiences of yourself and others, special events and holidays, various readings, and the mass media.

Record your ideas when you get them and plan ahead what you will preach. Look and listen for material that will support these sermon ideas.

It is exciting to receive an idea and see it grow and develop into a finished sermon. A preacher's joy in ministry increases when he develops ideas from his own spiritual life, study, and ministry to people.

REACTION AND RESPONSE

As an experiment, maintain a notebook for two weeks. Divide the page into two columns. Title one column "Idea" and title one column "Resource." As you get ideas for sermons, list them. As the ideas mature in your thinking move each to a separate page and note related thoughts. Develop as led.

Chapter 8
A Text for the Sermon

George Sweazy told of being the guest speaker at an old church in Komarno, Czechoslovakia. When he stepped to the pulpit, the people stood. He greeted the people and paused, but they remained standing. The preacher started his sermon and after a few minutes again paused. The people still stood. Sweazy turned to his translator and asked, "Don't they want to sit down?" The translator looked puzzled, but spoke to the people and they all took their seats. The preacher later discovered it was the custom of the people to stand until the preacher gave his text from God's word. Sweazy commented, "Perhaps the congregation is unwilling to settle down and listen until they are sure they will get to hear the Bible."[1] Selecting a Scripture for your sermons is a very important part of sermon preparation. By always selecting a text, you are more likely to do biblical preaching.

THE IDEA AND THE TEXT

Which comes first, the idea or the text? It doesn't matter, although I find sermon preparation develops easier from a text. God might give you an idea, and then you will seek a text to support it. You may read a Scripture passage and then receive from God an idea for a sermon. Both ways become useful to you. The important thing is that the idea and the text agree with one another. Additional study will determine this.

The sermon text is the selection of Scripture which contains or supports the idea of the sermon. Each sermon should have a text. The word "text" comes from a word which means "product of weaving." A weaver begins with an idea for a design. On the loom is first placed the basic thread and between these threads other colors are woven to produce the design. The weaver runs the different colors back and forth through the basic background thread. Soon the planned design will be produced. The sermon text is the basic biblical "thread" containing an idea. The preacher weaves in interpretations of the text, illustrations, and applications to life and presents a message from the Lord.

The text and the idea are united in what Pastor Dean Dickens called a "marriage."[2] In this marriage of text and idea, the text is always the stronger partner. The idea and the text must have the same central thought; both must be about the same subject. Phillips Brooks noted, "Never draw out of a text a meaning which you know is not there. If your text has not your truth in it, find some other text which has. If you can find no text for your idea in the Bible, then preach on something else."[3]

The text can supply general support for a specific idea. Clarence Macartney preached a famous sermon on 2 Timothy 4:9, 21.[4] Paul asked Timothy to "come before winter . . . do your best to come soon." The sermon idea was to make spiritual decisions now while we have time. The text supports the idea and supplies some illustrations for the sermon. Paul wanted Timothy to visit him soon because in winter no boats journeyed to Rome. Those who tried often failed to make the dangerous trip. If Timothy waited until after winter, Paul would probably be gone. Paul felt he would soon be killed by his captors (v. 6). The idea and the text jointly supported the theme, "act now while the opportunity is available."

A student had this idea for a sermon: "Boldness is essential in preaching the Word of God." To find a text he looked in the concordance under the word "bold." He chose Proverbs 28:1: "The wicked flee when no man pursues: but the righteous are bold as a lion." The last part of the verse seems to support the idea. However, the text and the idea would have a very weak marriage. Proverbs 28:1 doesn't refer to preaching but to the way sin makes one feel guilty and afraid. A person without sin is bold and doesn't run with shame or guilt. A better text for the preacher's idea would be Acts 4:13–17. The passage mentions "boldness" three times, and the text describes Christians as preaching the Word with courageous boldness. The idea and this text have a strong "marriage."

There are several advantages of preaching from a text. Such preaching shows our calling to preach the Word of God. If you get into the habit of preaching without a text, you may begin to see your job as just a speaker and not a preacher of God's truth. Like Paul, you are a "chosen vessel" to carry God's Word to all people (Acts 9:15). Authority and confidence will be added to the message when you use a text, if you use it correctly. Your personal ideas and other teachings will be judged by the text.

The use of a text gives you an opportunity to study and explain a passage of Scripture. When the Bible is related to life, the hearers are encouraged to study the Bible privately.

Understanding the message improves when a text is used. Most of the people will have a Bible and can read the text. A text encourages unity, and the people have a reminder of the message.

SELECTING A TEXT

In selecting sermon texts, do not neglect any part of the Bible, for all Scripture is inspired and useful. Variety comes by preaching from all the Bible. Every preacher has favorite sections of the Bible. Be aware that you may be using these many times and neglecting other Scriptures which would make excellent sermon texts.

You will certainly want to select a text that captures your interest. If you are not enthusiastic about the passage, you will probably not interest the people. An appropriate sermon text meets four standards. It (1) has a clear meaning, (2) contains a complete and suitable unit of thought, (3) is faithful to the context, and (4) meets the needs of people.

A Text with Clear Meaning

Choose a text that can be clearly understood with basic interpretation and illustration. Some Scriptures seem strange and curious and to use them only creates curiosity. Spiritual needs remain unmet by using these texts, although they may indulge fanciful ideas of interpreters who claim to have "hidden wisdom" that sees beyond the obvious to some hidden meaning. Where Cain got his wife (Gen. 4:17) makes interesting speculation but provides little "spiritual food."

A Scripture should never be treated as an allegory unless the Scripture claims that for itself. An allegory is a story which contains a hidden special meaning. People, places, or things are used as symbols to represent deeper truths. Galatians 4:21–31 uses Sara and Hagar as symbols of two relationships before God. Paul states "which things are symbolic. For these are the two covenants" (v. 24).

Acts 9:17–26 was the text for a missions sermon entitled "A Window, a Basket, and a Rope." The passage describes Paul's rescue from his enemies. "The disciples took him by night and let him down through the wall in a large basket." The preacher said, "the window in Acts 9 symbolizes a view of the world. In the matter of missions, we need to pray that God would give us a window, a vision." The basket was interpreted as the church and the rope as believers. The clear meaning of the text has nothing to do with any of these truths. The passage clearly shows how God watches over his servants. The window doesn't symbolize anything; it was only an opening through which Paul was let down. The basket doesn't represent the church. It was only a means of getting Paul to the ground without injury! This passage could be used for a sermon on God's care of his servants. God manifests His care through the people in the church. The believers who rescued Paul were church members who showed commitment, tenacity, and courage. The text was used inappropriately, treated as an allegory with special hidden meaning. Select a text with clear meaning; do not add meanings that are not present unless the text gives it special meaning.

A Complete Unit of Thought

Select a text with a complete unit of thought. Jesus' words to Judas, "Whatever you do, do quickly" (John 13:27) mean nothing separated from the rest of the passage of which it is a part. Many verses can be used by themselves, such as John 3:16. Other verses are incomplete unless joined with the verse before or after. Translators placed verse numberings in the text when the Bible was translated into English. Sometimes the verse numbers break a complete unit of thought. Always be sure to select a text with a complete unit of thought. Usually a paragraph will contain a complete unit of thought.

Choose a Scripture text long enough to develop a complete sermon. Again, some verses like John 3:16 contain so much truth that several messages can be developed from the one verse. Most sermons will need several verses to have enough material for a complete passage. If you use a long Scripture text, the sermon may be too long and hard to follow. Of course, every idea in a long passage should not be developed in a sermon. Develop only one key idea from a selected text.

Faithful to the Context

The text must be used as it relates to the context, the Scripture surrounding the text. The verse is part of a paragraph. Paragraphs make up a chapter or section. The section is contained in a book or letter. A book is located either in the Old or New Testament. Each part of the context influences the text, and the text must never be divorced from the context.

Romans 13:11–14 was chosen for an evangelistic sermon. The text was applied to unbelievers. The surrounding Scripture shows the passage was written to believers. Romans was written to those "called to be saints" (1:7), and Romans 12:1 introduces the last section of the book, which is an appeal to the "brothers." These are Christians, and Paul asks them to be fully dedicated to Christ. Romans 13:11 notes they had "already believed." The text should be developed toward believers who should be asked to rededicate their lives, turn from sin, and live for Christ.

When choosing a sermon text be faithful to the context, choose a complete unit of thought, and stay with the clear meaning of the passage. Does this outline reflect a suitable use of the text?

Walking in the Light (Rom. 13:11–14)
Paul gives three steps to right living for Christians.
I. Christian, wake up (v. 11). Realize your condition. Realize Christ may come back soon, so get to work and win the world.
II. Christian, put aside sin (vv. 12–13). When a Christian sins, Christ is dishonored and the Christian's witness is weakened.
III. Christian, put on Christ-likeness (v. 14). Instead of sin, be clothed with Christ.

Faithfulness to the context means that one verse must not be taken as stating something different than is taught by the entire passage. Some use Acts 2:38 to teach that baptism washes away sin and therefore is essential for salvation. A sermon with that idea and with Acts 2:38 as the only text is using the verse as a proof-text. The context states the people "accepted his message" (v. 41). That describes faith exercised before baptism. Peter also said, "Repent, then, and turn to God, so that your sins may be wiped out, that times of refreshing may come from the Lord" (Acts 3:19). Clyde Fant noted, "Every cult and heresy from the first century on has been long on proof-texts and short on authentic interpretations."[5]

An appropriate text will have a clear meaning and contain a complete and suitable unit of thought. The use of the text must be faithful to the context. A final guideline is equally important.

Relevant to People

The text must be relevant to the needs of the people. A text may be very interesting to you, but will it help the people to whom you preach? You may have read some new book on a biblical passage. You are eager to share these new ideas with your people. Are they mature enough for the message? Should you first preach on a theme that prepares them? Select a text which relates to the needs of the people. "Just because a sermon is couched in the latest idiom and addressed to a contemporary situation does not make it truly relevant. To be genuinely relevant, it must be addressed to man's ultimate spiritual need. . . . Only the preaching of the Gospel is preaching that is truly relevant."[6]

A sermon idea and a text are the beginnings of a message from God's Word. Now we will study how to interpret the text. Interpretation needs illustration and application to help the understanding. All of this material must be presented in a way that will help the people to understand the message and make appropriate decisions.

REACTION AND RESPONSE

Haddon Robinson stresses finding the "Big Idea" in the text. Study this principle in *Biblical Preaching*, 31–48.

Chapter 9
Interpreting the Text

You have a text, what next? The text must be interpreted, probably the most important step in preparing a sermon. It must always be preceded with prayer. The Lord has promised the Holy Spirit will guide us to the truth. The sermon must say what the text teaches. The Bible contains "some things hard to understand" (2 Peter 3:16). Careful interpretation prevents you from unintentionally distorting the Word of God. Paul's testimony is what we strive for, "Nor do we distort the word of God" (2 Cor. 4:2 NIV). Pray and study for a true interpretation.

The Bible is a spiritual "library," a collection of sixty-six different books written by individuals who "spoke as they were moved by the Holy Spirit" (2 Pet. 1:21). The Holy Spirit inspired the Scriptures and is active in the work of interpreting the Scriptures. Jesus promised the Holy Spirit's guidance in our search for the truth (John 15:13). Paul gave assurance that the Holy Spirit helps us understand "the things that have been freely given to us by God" (1 Cor. 2:12). Depend upon the Holy Spirit to guide you in your study of Scripture.

The unity of the Bible encourages interpretation. Jesus described this unity, "These are the Scriptures . . . which testify of me" (John 5:39). Jesus Christ gives unity to the Bible. The Old Testament points to His coming; the New Testament unfolds His work for the salvation of all people. Every interpretation should support this basic theme of the Bible.

John Stott[1] likened preaching to building a bridge between the past and the present. By interpretation the preacher discovers the Scripture's original meaning and applies it to life today.

```
                    PREACHING
  Meaning of    /\    /\    /\    Application for
   the Past    /  \  /  \  /  \    the Present
━━━━━━━━━━━━━┻━━━━┻━━━━┻━━━━┻━━━━━━━━━━━━━━
```

A civil engineer knows bridge building involves work. Bible interpretation requires study, creative thinking, and faith. The process rewards the preacher with material to build a stronger biblical sermon.

INTERPRETING THE SERMON BY INDUCTIVE BIBLE STUDY

A valuable method of interpretation is an Inductive Bible Study. This study examines a text to discover the general truths it contains. "Inductive" means moving from specific to general. So in an Inductive Bible Study (IBS), we begin with studying specific details to find the general truths of the passage of Scripture. Farrar Patterson points out, "The IBS is a method of getting into the Bible for yourself without becoming a slave to the writings or interpretations of others."[2] IBS is done before you consult any commentaries. With only your Bible, you will pray and let the Holy Spirit guide you to a deeper understanding of the text and its application.

Deductive Bible study begins with the commentaries and allows their conclusions to guide the message. The inductive approach encourages independent study as the first step to understanding the text. IBS develops faith and a more effective prayer life. You depend on the Lord's revelation more than what you read in a commentary. A personal encounter with the Lord through the Word will be your best preparation to proclaim the Word. Through IBS you permit the Lord to speak to you before you speak to the people.

Although I consider the IBS an excellent tool for sermon preparation, it is only a beginning point and must be used with caution. John C. Cooper asks,

> Isn't this an invitation to leave orthodoxy? May not one devise his own "theology," as we see done by Jim Jones, David Koresh, Moses David (The Children of God) and many other cultists? I think IBS would be good for one well grounded in theology but not for others. There are other spirits beside the Holy Spirit. We see the effects of these unholy spirits all around us. It is surely the reason human prejudices are often preached and declared

Interpreting the Text 61

to be from God's Word. It is sobering to read sermons from the 19th century that defend slavery as biblical![3]

Begin sermon preparation with an inductive study on the chosen passage but always follow up with other study approaches that will check out your personal ideas.

Inductive Bible Study improves your mental ability by thought and imagination. If you get your sermons from someone else, your creative ability will decrease. Muscles must be used or they weaken. Imagination and mental creativeness improve as you use them.

An Inductive Bible Study has four parts:

1. The Scripture passage
2. Observations
3. Questions
4. Text Ideas/Application

Let's examine the method of an IBS by doing one on 2 Thessalonians 1:3–4.

Scripture Passage

Begin your study by reading the text many times, depending on the Holy Spirit to guide you into truth. I have found it helpful to write the Scripture, a phrase at a time, in a column at the edge of a blank piece of paper. This provides room for notes. Write the translation you will use in the pulpit. Using your pulpit text will make it familiar to you. Wait until later to compare other translations because these affect your interpretation. Do not write the phrases of the text too close together. You will want room to underline key words and make notations. Some find it helpful to use different-colored pencils to connect phrases or emphasize important words.

Sample Scripture:

> We are bound
> to thank God always
> for you, brethren,
> as it is fitting
> because your faith
> grows exceedingly
> and the love
> of every one of you all
> abounds
> toward each other

Write the entire text. What you leave out may be a key word which can change your entire interpretation.

Wayne McDill[4] suggested a "structural diagram" to gain an overview of the text. This tool "is a phrase-by-phrase chart of the text in the exact word order of the translation you use. Its purpose is to show in graphic form the relationship of various ideas in the text." Start with the first independent clause. Main ideas are placed on the left and secondary clauses go to the right. The result will show equal ideas lined up vertically. Place connectives in brackets. A structural diagram of 2 Thessalonians 1:3–4 looks like this.

We are bound to thank God
                always
                for you brethren
                as it is fitting
      (because) your faith grows exceedingly
           (and)
                the love abounds toward each other
                      of every one of you
(so that)
We boast of you
                among the churches of God
                for your patience
                (and) faith
                      in all your persecutions
                          (and) tribulations

Notice three equal phrases relate to the way Paul gives thanks to God: always, for you brethren, as it is fitting. Prayer is a continuing experience which focuses on God, has concern for others, and is certainly fitting for a Christian. The connective "because" refers back to Paul's prayer of thanks. Why does he thank God? Two ideas are lined up equally in the diagram: faith grows and love abounds.

Observations

Beside the Scripture write down observations you make about the text. Closely observe every part of the text. Consider the verb tenses. As you observe the text, another Scripture may come to your mind; put it down. Later you will use your concordance to locate cross-references which will help explain a word used by the writer. What are the key words? If you do not know a word meaning, look it up in your dictionary. Does the word have a theological meaning you will not find in your dictionary? For words you understand, try

Interpreting the Text

and think of other words to explain them. In 2 Thessalonians 1:3, "brethren" reminds us of family. Paul thinks of the church as a family of faith, and he is thankful for them.

These are some other observations I noted in my Inductive Bible Study of 2 Thessalonians 1:3–4. Thanksgiving is a part of prayer. We may not always agree with each other, but we can be thankful God uses everyone in the family of faith. Paul is thankful for this in the church—faith grows, love abounds, patience/faith remains in persecutions. Some church members are faithful in attendance, but their faith does not grow. They have no faith to witness, give, serve. A church full of love! And it is growing. Love shows we are disciples. Love increases where faith grows—faith in Christ and faith in each other. The Thessalonian church is being talked about. Every church has a reputation. This church was known for patience in persecution. They were willing to suffer for what they believe.

Does the passage contain contrasts or comparisons? Consider the significance of repetition in the passage. Observe connecting words such as "and," "because," "therefore." These mean you should relate one part to another. Write your observations next to the part of the verse to which it applies. Do not overlook the paragraphs before and after your text. The context affects the meaning.

Use your imagination on the observation part of the IBS. Try to place yourself in the setting. Close your eyes and think about what is happening. Write down what you "see."

This part of the IBS has been called the "chicken yard" phase. As Wayne McGill explained, "Every country boy knows what happens when you throw a large piece of bread into a chicken yard. The chickens pounce on the bread en masse and tear it into pieces. If one runs off with a fragment large enough to be seen, two or three others will give chase and peck away at it. Finally, the entire piece of bread is broken up into tiny segments. That's what you want to do to the Bible passage—take it apart into its smallest segments in order to see what is there."[5]

Don't rush this part of the Inductive Bible Study. Examine it in detail and then leave it for a while. When you look at it again, new relationships will probably be seen.

Questions

The third part of the IBS asks questions about the text. Some of these will surface during the observation step but try to hold them until you "see" as much as possible in the text. Ask all you can think of. Write your questions in an adjoining column or on another page for later study. Who? What? Why?

Where? When? and How? should be asked about the text. How did he feel? Why did he do this? In 2 Thessalonians 1:3–4, the first word is "we." Who is this? Look at the context. Verse one tells you the answer, "Paul, Silas and Timothy." Who is "you, brothers"? Verse one says "to the church of the Thessalonians." Questions create ideas and help you see relationships in the text and begin to make applications.

I asked these questions in my IBS on the passage. Does thanksgiving for people make us more understanding and patient with them? What keeps our faith growing? Why do church members need faith since they are already forgiven and accepted by God? Faith to do what? Do we love each other? Why does our love not grow? How can love grow to include "everyone" in the church, especially those I don't like or know they are doing wrong? Does love include forgiveness? What reputation does our church have? What is being said about our church? Why do some Christians give up and others persevere? What trials were the Thessalonians facing? Did persecution come to them from government? Unbelievers? Within the church?

Patterson cautions about answering questions too quickly. "As soon as one starts answering questions, he stops asking them. The more the questions, the richer the interpretation. The questions are the link between observation and interpretation."[6]

Text Ideas/Application

Think about the application of the verse to your church. How does this verse relate to us? Be careful to see the relationship between all the verses of the passage. Some have seen an idea in one verse, but it may not be supported by the entire text. Put down every idea that comes to your mind. You may develop some of them later. Describe the central thought of the passage in your own words. What principle was at work in the original event that continues to be needed today? Note possible outlines, illustrations, or themes. Do not prematurely impose a sermon outline on the passage; you are still discovering the meaning of the text. Much more exciting work needs to be done on the passage. An idea may ignite your preaching fervor, but it must be checked for accuracy in the remaining study time.

An Inductive Bible Study should be your first study after choosing a text to preach. Other materials such as commentaries and sermon books will be helpful, but consult them only after you do your own Bible study.

You may have had an idea, chosen a text, done an IBS on the text, completed the additional study described in the remainder of this chapter, and found out the Scripture didn't support your idea. What then? Find another text that supports your idea or preach on one of the ideas discovered in your Bible study.

Interpreting the Text

Study the Scripture first—just you, your Bible, and the Lord seeking the meaning for your people. Timothy was told, "Be diligent to present yourself approved to God, a worker who does not need to be ashamed, rightly dividing the word of truth" (2 Tim. 2:15). An Inductive Bible Study requires work. It takes time to work through each verse. I strongly encourage you to devote plenty of quality study time to the IBS. Begin your preparation on Monday. You will also need time for ideas to mature. Developing skill in an IBS will be one of the most productive periods of your sermon preparation. The Scripture will become part of you, and the message will be delivered with more enthusiasm, conviction, and relevance.

An Inductive Bible Study encourages you to develop your own ideas. As I thought about these two verses from 2 Thessalonians, five different ideas came to me. The observations and questions will provide support for these ideas. Of course, much more work will be needed to develop them into messages. Always keep your Bible study notes. You will want them again when you preach from the passage.

DIGGING DEEPER INTO THE WORD

The Inductive Bible Study, a first step in interpreting the text, will help you begin to understand the text and will probably give you new ideas. After the IBS, the text should be examined more closely. Four other studies will add more material to your sermon file. These studies often need the help of additional library resources, especially dictionary and concordance. These four interpretation studies are (1) a study of the words and their relationships, (2) a study of the context, (3) a study of the type of writing, (4) a study of parallel references. Completing these studies is like digging deeper into the earth in search of precious minerals. God blesses those who work to better understand His Word! In Bible study, digging into the text always produces valuable results. What should you study as you dig into the text?

Study the Words and Their Relationship

To properly interpret the Bible you must study the words in the text and how they relate to each other. Words in the Greek language have different meanings. The position of the word in the sentence shows how it should be emphasized. These are just two reasons why the study of words and their relationship affects interpretation.

For example, Romans 3:23–25 is frequently used for evangelistic sermons. Word study provides a better interpretation of the passage. Some key words in these verses which must be understood are italicized.

> Since all have *sinned* and fall short of the glory of God, they are *justified* by his *grace* as a gift, through the *redemption* which is in Christ Jesus whom God put forward as an *expiation* by his blood, to be received by *faith*. This was to show God's *righteousness*.
> Romans 3:23–25 RSV

All of these words are theological, describing mankind's relationship to God. Their meaning in the Bible differs sharply from what they mean to an unbeliever. Part of your work as a preacher is to study these words. You must be able to help an unbeliever or a new Christian to understand them.

This passage has three words which describe Christ's work of salvation. How are people saved? Paul says they are "*justified* . . . through the *redemption* which is in Christ Jesus . . . as an *expiation*." Using these three words in a sermon as they are is like trying to get a child to swallow three BIG pills of medicine. Word study reveals that these words were common in Paul's day. "Justified" was used at the courthouse as a legal term to describe a judge declaring the guilty criminal just and releasing him, "just as if he had never sinned." "Redemption" was a marketplace word. A slave on the auction block could be purchased (redeemed) and set free. Christ's death paid the price to set us free from the slavery of sin and death. "Expiation" was a religious word heard in the temple. It referred to the place where the blood was sprinkled and forgiveness was sought. Jesus is the one where we find forgiveness and salvation from sin.

Word relationships are important for interpretation. Look again at Romans 3:23–25 and notice these words: "they," "which," "whom," "this." Each of these words relates to another part of the verse. The phrases begun by these words explain another part of the verse. "They" refers to all sinners. "Which" relates to redemption. "Whom" means Christ Jesus. "This" relates back to all the preceding section—Christ's death on the cross. Including definitions of the three key words, the expanded meaning of the passage can be read:

> Since all have sinned and fall short of the glory of God, (all sinners) are declared just by his grace as a gift, through the redemption which is in Jesus. Jesus was put forward by God as the one who forgives by his blood, to be received by faith. This death of Christ for all sinners shows God's righteousness.

New translations come as a result of word study. Comparing translations is helpful for interpreting the text. Notice the different interpretation in these two translations of Romans 8:28. The translations place a different word as subject of the second clause.

Interpreting the Text

(a) *And we know that all things work together for good to them that love God, to them who are the called according to his purpose.*

(b) *We know that in everything God works for good with those who love him, who are called according to his purpose.*

What is the subject in translation "a"? "All things work together for good." In translation "b" God is the subject. "God works for good." The Greek language supports the second translation; our life experience does also. Everything doesn't always work out for the good, but God will certainly work in everything for good if we let Him! The study of words and their relationship is an invaluable tool for interpreting the Scripture.

A few resources will aid your word study. *Strong's Exhaustive Concordance of the Bible* lists the Greek and Hebrew words which are translated by the English in your text. A Bible dictionary defines theological words, and also lists other places to look in the Bible for the use of the word. Word-study books such as *Vine's Expository Dictionary of Biblical Words* are helpful tools. Some of these give the way Bible words were used in everyday life at the time the Scripture was written. Commentaries on the book you are studying usually include word studies.

Study the words in 2 Thessalonians 1:3–4, the text of our earlier Inductive Bible Study. *Vine's* lists nine Greek words under "grow." One of these is translated "grows exceedingly" in 2 Thessalonians 1:3. The word is formed from the root "to grow or increase" and the prefix "over." *Vine's* notes the word "is used of faith and love in their living and practical effects. Lightfoot compares this verb and the next in the verse (*pleonazo*, "to abound") in that the former implies 'an internal, organic growth, as of a tree,' the latter 'a diffusive, or expansive character, as of a flood irrigating the land.'"[7] The Thessalonians' internal resource of faith grew as their love spread to others. The picture language from the commentary offers possibilities for later sermon development.

Study the Context

There are three different types of context study. First, the written context is the verses which go before or follow the text. These are the verses to which the text is connected. The verses are also related to a section within the book. The book is part of either the Old or New Testament. In previous lessons we have seen the importance of the context.

The most common error of interpretation occurs when one verse is given a meaning without checking the relationship to the meaning found in the surrounding material. In 1 Corinthians 2:9 Paul quotes from Isaiah 40. A common interpretation cites this as a reference to heaven, "Eye has not seen, nor ear heard, Nor have entered into the heart of man the things which God has prepared for those who love him." Check the context (vv. 6–15). Paul writes about spiritual wisdom. God's wisdom is hidden at first from unbelievers, but now "God has revealed it to us by his Spirit" (v. 10).

The historical context is the second type of context study. When you study a passage, look for facts about the place or the people mentioned. They can be important in understanding the text. According to 1 Thessalonians 1:7–8, the Thessalonian church was known "in every place." This truth becomes more understandable when we know Thessalonica was a port city on a main trade route. The most important road between Rome and the east went through the town. Travellers and pilgrims filled the city. What an exciting place for a church. They succeeded in building a witnessing fellowship, and the word spread down that main route to people "everywhere."

Social context is the last context study. Jesus asked a Samaritan woman for a drink; she expressed surprise. The writer, John, provided a word of social context, "For Jews have no dealing with Samaritans" (John 4:9). Checking some historical resources will tell you the Samaritans were half-breeds and despised by Jews as an unclean people. The text shows Jesus' love for all people.

Faithful interpretation requires contextual study. The material surrounding the text should begin this study. Historical and social contexts also provide information helpful to the interpretation.

Study the Type of Writing

The Bible contains several different types of writing including law, history, poetry, prophecy, biography, and letters. Books with these categories share some characteristics which the interpretation should consider. Some of the poetry is written in "parallel" lines, so that one line explains the other. The writings of the prophets are written differently from that of the psalmists.

The Scripture writers used other types of writing to make it more interesting. A parable is used in writing and speaking to teach truth. A parable has been defined as an "earthly story with a heavenly meaning."[8] A parable makes only one point and all the details emphasize one main truth. An allegory is a story in which each detail has a meaning. Jesus used many parables (Mark 4:34); it was his favorite method of teaching. Parables must be interpreted differently than allegories.

Other figures of speech were used by Scripture writers. These are literary devices which describe or illustrate. A simile compares two things by using the words "as" or "like." Revelations 1:12–16 contains many similes to describes Jesus. In the NKJV the word "like" is used five times in the passage. A metaphor compares two things without using "as" or "like." Christians are called the "salt of the earth . . . the light of the world"

(Matt. 5:13–14). John's gospel uses many metaphors for Jesus: bread of life, door, the good shepherd, etc. A paradox is a figure of speech which makes two true statements that seem to contradict each other. Matthew 16:25 and 1 John 2:7–8 are examples of paradox. A hyperbole exaggerates to teach a truth. Jesus used this literary device when he asked, "Why do you look at the speck in your brother's eye, but do not perceive the plank in your own eye?" (Luke 6:41).

Sometimes the Bible writer denotes if the writing is a figure of speech. John did this (John 2:19, 21–22). Paul also tells us when he used an allegory (Gal. 4:24). At other places, common sense guides your interpretation. At the Last Supper Jesus gave the disciples bread, saying, "Take, eat; this is my body," and then a cup, "Drink from it, all of you. For this is my blood of the covenant" (Matt. 26:26–28). This is symbolic or metaphorical language. Jesus used other metaphors: "I am the door"; "I am the light." He meant these as figures of speech to describe His work.

Figures of speech make writing more interesting. They must be considered when interpreting the text.

Study the Parallel Rreferences

A helpful step in interpreting the text is to study other references in the Bible which use the same word. A concordance is your resource for this interpretation study. An interlinear translation, which places the Greek above the English, becomes useful in determining the Greek root word. These are listed in better concordances and refer to the exact place that root is used. A concordance can't tell you the context of the word. You must read and carefully determine if the word is used in a similar context.

The Inductive Bible Study of 2 Thessalonians 1:3–4 noted the idea of a "growing faith." The context revealed that this was written to the church at Thessalonica. The "faith" refers to the quality of the Christian life. Church members with strong working "faith" is the idea; the idea is not the initial commitment involved in salvation. With this context in mind, turn to your concordance for parallel references.

The New Testament lists over 226 references to faith! Not all of them will support your idea because many of them refer to salvation. Look for references which relate to faith at work in a church. First, see if there are other references in the book of Thessalonians. Parallel references in the same book as your text will usually carry the same context and interpretation. These parallel references are in 1 Thessalonians 1:3, 8; 3:2, 10; and 5:8. Second Thessalonians 3:2 refers to faith, but it relates to the faith response of a new believer and thus would not be used in your sermon. Only use references that support your idea.

Now look for references in other writings of Paul that illustrate a church with strong faith. In Romans 1:8 Paul makes a similar compliment about the church at Rome. Second Corinthians 10:15 speaks of a growing faith that will result in expanded mission work. Colossians 2:6 challenges a church to grow in faith. The church at Thyatira was commended for its "love and faith" (Rev. 2:19). All of these references were found with a concordance. Each reference was studied to see if it fit the context of the sermon idea.

The study of parallel references usually produces more material than you can use. Select which verses give the strongest support to your idea. Your research may produce ideas which can be used another time in a different sermon. Be sure to write these ideas down for future use.

Four studies will help you interpret a chosen text in preparation for preaching. Study the words and their relationship. Study the context. Study the type of writing and the parallel references. At the conclusion of the Inductive Bible Study, and these four interpretation studies, you should be able to write the main idea of the text. Now begin gathering other material to explain and illustrate it. Sometimes these studies cause a change in the sermon idea. Your original idea may not be supported by the text. Interpretation should result in a stronger idea closely related to the text.

REACTION AND RESPONSE

Complete an Inductive Bible Study on Luke 14:25–27. What is the primary theme of this passage on which you can build a sermon? Do any words require additional study? How does verse 26 relate to the preceding context? Are there parallel references which help you understand "carry his cross and follow me"?

Do additional study in this very helpful book on Bible interpretation: J. Robertson McQuilkan, *Understanding and Applying the Bible* (Chicago: Moody Press, 1983), especially the guidelines and skills found on pages 61–165.

Unit 4

Organizing the Message

During the time this book was being prepared for printing, several construction projects were underway on our campus. Each of these involved time, money, and the labor of many volunteers and employees. Before any work started, plans were prepared and decisions made to determine our objective and the type of structure we wanted the finished product to look like. Preparing to preach is a construction project in which the preacher, under the leadership of the Spirit, builds a sermon.

Thus far in this process of building we have chosen an idea and interpreted a text which embodies that idea. At other times you will be led to a text first and, after interpretation, decide which main thought of the passage will be your sermon. Now answer the basic question, "where will this sermon go?" This is a question of objectives. Every sermon needs direction—where are we going? That famous person "Anonymous" said, "The person who isn't going anywhere usually gets there." Objectives tell the direction of the sermon. The sermon must be concerned with some major area of life and should have a specific goal for the listeners.

A lack of clear objectives is a common weakness in preaching. Remember, biblical preaching appeals "to the hearers to respond positively to the will of God." Objectives state the desired response and are essential for effective preaching.

Objectives state the direction of the sermon. The sermon "building" has an introduction, a body, and a conclusion. The structure has windows, illustrations that help to see the truth. The preacher puts all of this together in an arrangement that will interest people and appeal to them.

Lessons 11–19 take us through this construction process. An architect learns how to draw plans and has freedom to design different structures. I never much liked housing developments where all the houses are of the same design. Your sermons should have variety, and as a preacher you have the freedom to design and build sermons suitable to the needs of your congregation. Remember, the Lord is the Master Designer and will lead you in building the sermon.

Chapter 10
Preaching Objectives

Each sermon should have an objective. The objective is the aim of the sermon, the purpose of the message. What is your desired result in preaching the message? Without objectives, sermons are religious talk with little impact. Unless sermons have an aim, preachers become like the Athenians who "spent their time in nothing else but either to tell or to hear some new thing" (Acts 17:21). Preaching has three levels of objectives: The total objective, the major objective, and the specific objective.

THE TOTAL OBJECTIVE

The overall purpose of ministry is that others might "have life, and have it more abundantly" (John 10:10). Preaching, one part of the ministry, shares this total objective, to bring life to people. Any sermon becomes appropriate by presenting people with the life known in Jesus Christ. The total objective of preaching, therefore, is abundant life.

THE MAJOR OBJECTIVE

Major objectives relate to some general issues of life. Every person is concerned for life, but there are different life needs. A major objective focuses on a particular area of life. Determining this major objective for the message helps maintain unity and provides direction. There are six major objectives for sermons you will preach. Four of these receive closer study in succeeding lessons.

1. Evangelistic—sermons which seek to bring the unsaved to Jesus Christ and into the fellowship of the church.
2. Devotional—sermons which seek to move people to love, adore, and worship God.
3. Doctrinal—sermons which explain a specific Bible doctrine.
4. Ethical—sermons which apply Bible teachings on morality and daily life. The desired result is that people think, act, and live by Bible teachings.
5. Consecrative—sermons directed to believers asking for a deeper commitment to Christ and His work.
6. Pastoral—sermons that minister to people in crises and suffering, by giving hope, comfort, and encouragement.

These major objectives involve all the concerns of life. In a local church the pastor's preaching ought to include all these objectives. Using a variety of objectives helps you to speak to the various needs of the people.

A sermon idea developed from the Bible study of 2 Thessalonians 1:3–4 used the title, "A Church To Boast About," with these three divisions: A Church with Faith, A Church with Love, A Church with Patience. Since the sermon is directed to believers and asks "for a deeper commitment to Christ," it has a consecrative objective. It is possible to develop a three-part series on "Qualities of a Dynamic Church." Each sermon would be more topical with the Thessalonian church providing the basic model. The sermon on faith could have a doctrinal objective, the sermon on love an evangelistic objective, and the message on patience in suffering would emphasize a pastoral objective.

Form the habit of determining the major objective of each sermon you prepare. The major objective chosen reflects the target audience of the sermon. The evangelistic sermon aims at lost people or those outside the church fellowship. The consecrative message usually aims at church members. A devotional sermon aims at believers. Keep the material aimed in the direction of the major objective. Unity and force will be the result.

Some texts contain material suitable for more than one objective. Prayer, awareness of the people's needs, current events, personal interests, and other considerations will help you decide which objective you will follow. Acts 8:26–40 contains material supportive of more than one objective. I've heard sermons on the passage that mixed all these objectives together, and the end result was a weaker message. An evangelistic sermon can be developed with the focus on the Ethiopian's search for God and his commitment to Christ. A consecrative sermon on the Christian as soul-winner would use Philip as the primary reference. The text also contains material suitable for a doctrinal sermon on the Holy Spirit's role in evangelism.

THE SPECIFIC OBJECTIVE

Effective biblical sermons must have a specific objective. This objective states what you want the hearers to do after hearing the message. Remember our definition of preaching in chapter one: "Preaching is the proclamation of the good news of Jesus by one representing Christ, urgently appealing for the hearers to respond positively to the will of God." The specific objective states the response desired. It also states the target audience. It should be specific and grow out of the major objective.

The following specific objective was written for an evangelistic sermon on Romans 6:16–23: "To show what is meant by being a slave in Christ." The statement does not cite the target audience, nor does it state what the hearers are to do. The sermon lacked forceful appeal and clear direction because the preacher did not have a clearly defined objective. The specific objective might have been more clearly written: "that unbelievers would repent and reject the slavery of sin and receive freedom in Christ." Who?—"unbelievers"; do what?—"repent . . . receive freedom in Christ."

Luke 16:19–31 was the text for a sermon entitled "Life After Death" with this specific objective: "People might really know there is life after death." What people? What are they to do once they know this truth? The preacher wanted to preach an evangelistic sermon, but his objective does not seek an evangelistic result. A specific objective states: "That the lost will accept the gospel, trust Christ, and have certainty of life after death."

An evangelistic sermon, "The Searching God," based on Acts 8:26–39, had this specific objective: "That every lost sinner, especially the religious and self-righteous one, may realize their condition as a lost sinner and decide to receive Christ as their personal Lord and Savior as a response to the searching God." The objective, although somewhat wordy, is specific and states the desired response. Throughout the sermon the preacher spoke to "every lost sinner, especially to the religious and self-righteous ones."

A doctrinal sermon on baptism with the text Matthew 3:13–17 had this specific objective. "To elaborate to believers the significance of baptism and encourage them to be baptized, if not yet baptized." The major and specific objectives depend on each other and point to a specific group and response.

Objectives flow from the general to the specific. Each level is more specific. The relationship between the three levels of objectives could be pictured this way:

```
    \  TOTAL    /
     \ MAJOR   /
      \SPECIFIC/
       \      /
        \    /
         \  /
          \/
```

Consider the relationship between the major and specific objectives in these sermon outlines developed from Acts 8.

EVANGELISTIC OBJECTIVE

Joy on a Desert Road (Acts 8:26–40)
I. We search for life and joy (vv. 26–31).
II. Jesus is the end of our search for joy (vv. 32–35).
III. Decide for Jesus and discover joy in the desert (vv. 36–40).

Specific Objective: that unbelievers will accept Jesus Christ and experience the joy of salvation.

The major objective, body of the sermon, and specific objective are all united on the same theme, the need for salvation, and the target audience, unbelievers. The key word "joy" encourages unity in the message. In the next outline the title provides unity by repetition in each division.

CONSECRATIVE OBJECTIVE

A Successful Christian Witness (Acts 8:26–40)
I. A successful witness is sensitive to the Spirit's leadership (vv. 26–29).
II. A successful witness is familiar with the Scripture (vv. 30–34).
III. A successful witness always follows through (vv. 36–40).

Specific objective: that Christians will commit themselves to be soul-winners.

DOCTRINAL OBJECTIVE

The Holy Spirit's Role in Witnessing (Acts 8:26–40)
I. The Spirit convicts unbelievers (Ethiopian).
II. The Spirit directs believers (Philip).
III. The Spirit opens the mind to the Word (vv. 28–35).
IV. The Spirit completes the conversion (vv. 36–38).

Specific objective: to teach the role of the Holy Spirit in the preparation of a witnessing encounter, so that Christians will trust the power of the Holy Spirit and faithfully witness.

This doctrinal sermon outline requires additional Scripture to support the four truths, but the main idea comes from the text. The text provides illustration for each of the four parts. The doctrinal objective should result in action, and the specific objective should result in Christians going out to witness, trusting in the power of the Holy Spirit.

A sermon without objectives will be like a hunter who shoots into the air, with no game in sight, and who rarely hits any game. The gun has a sight, but the hunter must aim it at the desired target after loading the gun with the kind of ammunition suitable for the game. With practice, a hunter can hit the target and achieve his purpose. A preacher must aim his sermons at specific needs and load his messages with materials focused toward meeting those needs. The end result will be effective preaching and blessed lives.

REACTION AND RESPONSE

Based on your study of Luke 14:25–27, which major objective fits the passage? Write a specific objective for a sermon using this passage.

Chapter 11
Maintaining Unity in the Sermon

The Inductive Bible Study and other studies of the text will lead you to the basic meaning of the sermon text. Determine the target audience for that basic truth and what you want them to do. If the Scripture teaches several truths, decide on the one major theme you will emphasize in the message. The strongest sermons are united around one theme. Which major objective suits the theme you have chosen? With this central theme and major objective in mind, write a specific objective. The specific objective should answer these questions: Who is the sermon for? What do you want them to do? Once the specific objective is composed, you are ready to work on two other key elements, the thesis sentence and title. These two elements help support the unity of the message.

THE THESIS SENTENCE

The thesis sentence is the "key sentence of the sermon"; the sermon in one brief clear sentence. J. H. Jowett wrote, "I have a conviction that no sermon is ready for preaching . . . until we can express its theme in a short, pregnant sentence as clear as a crystal. . . . I do not think any sermon ought to be preached . . . until that sentence has emerged."[1] This sentence sets the direction of the sermon. Once heard, the people know what you plan to do. It should be stated early in the message, usually in the introduction. The thesis sentence can be effectively repeated at other places in the sermon. This supports the unity and keeps the theme before the people.

Maintaining Unity in the Sermon

Write and rewrite the thesis sentence until you have a clear, simple, and convincing statement. Cut out unnecessary words. Eight to fifteen words are enough to state the direction of the sermon. Make the sentence appeal to people. Work for a sentence with the quality of a proverb. The thesis sentence does not summarize the message points, nor does it tell how your theme is developed. The thesis states what the sermon is about.

The thesis sentence "will serve as a sort of magnet to keep one on the right track."[2] The body of the sermon explains, illustrates, and applies the truth of the thesis. The conclusion and invitation appeal for decisions based on the thesis.

The following sentences introduce a sermon on the New Testament disciple Demas. The message, "The Power to See It Through," used as texts Philemon 24, Colossians 4:14, and 2 Timothy 4:10.

> Concerning one character in the New Testament, mentioned only three times, one suspects that many Christians have not even heard of him—Demas. He illustrates one of the most familiar tragedies in human life—a fine beginning and a poor ending. He lacked the power to see it through.[3]

Either of the last two sentences served as the sermon thesis. At the very start of the message, the listeners know the sermon concerns the power to finish what we start. Later in the introduction, another sentence states the sermon theme in a more specific way. "I celebrate the qualities of faith and character that enable a man to see life through."

In the sermon, "The Shield of Faith," the thesis is stated as an opening question, asked immediately after the text is read.

> Above all, taking the shield of faith, wherewith we shall be able to quench all the fiery darts of the wicked (Eph. 6:16).

> But did the apostle who gives the counsel find his faith an all-sufficient shield?[4]

The question gives the direction of the sermon. The message will answer the question and show the adequacy of faith.

A Mother's Day message used 2 Kings 4:8–26. The thesis sentence read, "In these curious times, an inspiring example is needed for mothers—a pattern with which today's mothers might cut a new lifestyle from the fabric of life." The length of the sentence makes it cumbersome. A shorter one carried more force. "Mothers would do well to use this biblical pattern to cut a new lifestyle from the fabric of life." A more concise wording, "Mothers, here is a biblical pattern for a dramatically different lifestyle." The sermon will focus on the woman of Shunem described in the text and show her lifestyle. The conclusion and invitation will appeal to mothers to accept this biblical example.

"God can make dead things live," was the thesis sentence for a sermon based on Ezekiel 37:1–11. The thesis gave direction to the entire sermon as seen in the outline: (1) A dead home can live again, (2) A dead church can live again, (3) Dead sinners can live again. In the conclusion, the thesis was expanded to include the explanation made throughout the sermon. "Dead things can come to life when Jesus, God's own Son, comes to them."[5] The sermon would have been stronger with a more logical flow if the order of the points had been reversed, moving from sinner, home, to church. A dead sinner brought to life can change a home, and changed homes bring life to dead churches. In all three areas the presence of Jesus brings life.

An exposition of Ephesians 1:15–23 included this sentence in the introduction. "Too many Christians have never read the bank book to find out the vast spiritual wealth that God has put to their account through Jesus Christ."[6] The sentence incorporates a key phrase, "read the bank book," taken from the introductory illustration. The title uses this same phrase. A shorter version, followed by a sentence which relates to the illustration, packs more force. "Christians are wealthy but do not know it. They have never read their spiritual bank book." The sermon tells of the wealth Christians possess through Jesus Christ.

It is not easy to write the thesis sentence. "I find the getting of that sentence is the hardest, the most exacting, and the most fruitful labour in my study."[7] Your work to express the sermon theme in one short sentence will prove the effort worthwhile. Direction, unity, and appeal will result.

THE TITLE

One pastor acknowledged, "I've put everything I can into creating effective titles. I do it because I know unchurched people won't come, or come back, unless they can say, "Now that's something I want to hear about." The title . . . has to touch a genuine need or interest." Some series titles used in his ministry included, "God Has Feelings, Too," "Turning Houses into Homes," "Telling the Truth to Each Other," "Fanning the Flames of Marriage," and "Endangered Character Qualities."[8]

Titles are a familiar part of communication. Newspapers and magazines use titles. Newspaper headlines catch your attention in the grocery line. Movies and books use titles to advertise. A sermon title can be useful in your preaching ministry.

The title indicates the subject of the sermon. A good title creates interest. With it the listeners should know the direction of the sermon. Many people will remember the message by the title.

An effective title will meet these five specifications:

1. *Clear.* The title does not summarize the sermon. Instead, you group together a few words that clearly state what the sermon is about. Write a title that is clearly understood. Sometimes an element of intrigue may generate more interest, but guard against playing games with your titles.

2. *Accurate.* The sermon title should accurately describe the sermon objective and content. After preparing the sermon, check to see if the title really agrees with the message. If not, change the title. The sermon, "Why Join the Church?," must tell the reasons for joining the church. If the message focuses on the origin of the church the title is inaccurate.

3. *Limited.* Limit the title to the subject of the sermon. Do not include anything which you can't handle in the message. "The Power of the Resurrection" shows that the sermon will be limited to one aspect of the resurrection, although that is broad also. "The New Birth" is too broad for a suitable title or subject for one sermon. Limit it to some aspect of the new birth such as "Why Must I Be Born Again?"

4. *Brief.* Two to seven words are enough to state the topic and be interesting. One-word titles are usually too general. "Repentance" is much too general, broad, and unlimited. A better choice would be "Where Is Repentance Found?" Long titles are difficult to understand and hard to use in the message. "An Eschatological Perspective on the Sanctification of the Redeemed" sounds like a research paper instead of an exciting message.

5. *Suitable.* The title must be suitable for use in the pulpit. A sensational title detracts from the message. A sermon on Samson used the unsuitable title, "The Man Who Wouldn't Leave Women Alone." A message on the life of Hosea had the title, "In Love with a Prostitute." The title was accurate but too sensational.

The thesis sentence and the title are key elements in maintaining the unity of the sermon. Prepare these two tools after the text is interpreted and the specific objective is written. Each part depends on the other. Each of these components contain the same theme, aim toward the same audience, and move to achieve the same results. When this happens, the sermon will have unity and reach the purpose for which you prepared it.

REACTION AND RESPONSE

Write a thesis sentence and title for a sermon based on your study of Luke 14:25–27.

Chapter 12
Body Building

The preparation of your sermon has now come to the point of developing the main body of the sermon. Devote plenty of time to this before you prepare the introduction. You are better able to introduce somebody when you know him. After you have prepared the body of the sermon, you will know what to introduce. The body of the sermon explains, illustrates, and applies the sermon thesis. The body may have one or more points or divisions, but each must relate to one specific idea. Everything in the body must be supported by the text. The text and objective determine the body of the sermon.

MAJOR DIVISIONS

Martin Thielen, while editor of *Proclaim*, wrote, "These days, when I read, hear, or prepare a sermon, the question I ask is not, 'What are the points?' but 'What *is* the point?' I have a growing conviction that a good sermon should focus on one specific idea." He goes on to tell a story from Nora Delaney, a Pittsburgh insurance agent: "One of our training directors put on a fifteen-minute talk built around fourteen major points. A day after the speech, barely 30 percent of the audience could remember two of the points; fewer than two out of a hundred dredged up four. We conclude that, had the speaker covered fewer topics—say two major items—he would have been at least fifteen times more effective."[1]

The number of divisions in your sermon will vary depending on the text and the way you develop the idea. Do not form the habit of preparing every

Body Building 83

sermon with the same structure. Maintain a narrow focus, with every division supporting only one idea.

Galations 6:7–8 can be preached as a one-point sermon, "Sin Brings Destruction." The body of the message could contain the testimony of an Old Testament person (Bathsheba), a New Testament person (Ananias, Acts 5), and the testimony of someone today (Charles Colson). Each character explains, illustrates, and applies the one point.

The following week another sermon could be preached on the last part of the text, "The Spirit Brings Eternal Life." The same approach could be used, showing the truth of the text in Paul's life, in your life, or the life of another.

This text can also be developed as a two-point sermon, "Which Harvest Do You Desire?" One part would describe the harvest of the flesh and sin; the other part would focus on the harvest of the Holy Spirit.

Mark 2:1–12 tells of Jesus healing a paralytic. The text has many truths: people coming to Jesus (vv. 1–2); Jesus preaching the word (v. 2); faith in action (vv. 3–5); forgiveness of sin (vv. 5–11); Jesus the healer (v. 12); and Christ's authority versus the Pharisees/religion (vv. 6–10). It is possible to prepare several sermons from this text with each message focused on one theme. You must decide, under the leadership of the Spirit, on a specific theme and objective. Then develop the passage around the chosen theme.

The Inductive Bible Study of the text will provide many ideas and information. Your study may reveal many interesting details such as roof construction and what the men did to get the paralytic to Jesus. Verse five is a key verse, "When Jesus saw their faith, he said to the paralytic, 'Son, your sins are forgiven.'" To whom does "their" refer? Remember the study of words and their relationship? Does "their" refer only to the four men who carried the mat, or does it also include the man on the mat? I interpret the text to mean all five men. All of them had faith. What does the passage say about faith? Jesus healed a man in response to faith.

How can the sermon be developed? Decide first on an objective. Will you preach to Christians or to the lost? A doctrinal objective can be taken. The specific objective would state: "That believers understand the dual nature of faith; pray for and live by faith." A thesis sentence would state, "Like a coin, faith has two sides: faith in Jesus and the faith of Jesus." Draft a title which states the intention of the sermon. "Two Sides of Faith," "Jesus Looks for Faith," and "Does Jesus See Your Faith?" are possibilities.

The body of the sermon can be developed from the end of the text to the beginning.

    I. Faith in Jesus enables Him to change us.
       "Son, your sins are forgiven." He believed Jesus.

II. Living with the faith of Jesus enables Him to use us.
     The four men who carried the paralytic had the faith of Jesus.
     They walked by faith.
  III. Jesus looks for both sides of faith.
     "When he saw their faith." He desires the sinner saved.
     He desires his disciples to live by faith.

Evangelism can be the major objective of a sermon on this text. This objective would direct the message to the unsaved. The specific objective would read, "that all lost sinners would trust Christ, realizing faith in Jesus is necessary to have new life." The evangelistic objective now guides the divisions of the sermon. Arrange all material to emphasize the sinner—your target audience. Look at the text and see the progression of information about the paralyzed sinner: his condition (v. 3a); somebody cared about him (vv. 3b-4); he believed Jesus could help him and allowed himself to be brought to the house (vv. 3–4); he trusted his friends to open the roof and let him in (vv. 3–4); Jesus offered him forgiveness (v. 5); the man obeyed the Lord (v. 12). Verses 1–2 and 6–8 are concerned with secondary issues. Do not build major divisions out of them. These verses may supply supporting material for your major focus about the paralyzed man (sinner) and his decision.

A four-point evangelistic sermon could have this thesis: "It is possible to overcome the paralysis of sin." Possible titles are: "Walking Away From Sin," "Overcoming the Paralysis of Sin," or "How to Get Forgiveness of Sin." Each of these titles emphasizes words in the text. The sermon developed from the second title answers the question of how to overcome sin.

  Overcoming the Paralysis of Sin Happens When You:
    I. Accept your condition caused by sin (vv. 3–4).
   II. Follow the loving encouragement of those who care (vv. 3–5).
  III. Turn in faith to Jesus (vv. 3–5, 11).
   IV. Obey Jesus now and overcome sin (v. 12).

The title can be used whenever you introduce a new division. The divisions can also utilize key words of your title.

   I. You must acknowledge sin's paralysis.
  II. Others want you to overcome the paralysis of sin.
  III. Jesus has power to overcome your paralysis.
  IV. You will overcome sin when you trust and obey Jesus.

A consecrative sermon on this same text has this specific objective: "That believers will accept their soul-winning responsibility and commit themselves to bring lost people to Jesus." The thesis: "Am I a channel for Christ's forgiveness?" This sermon focuses on the four men who carried the paralytic to Jesus. They are examples of faithful Christian witnesses. Their concern for a lost friend was a link in the man's salvation experience. Suggested titles include: "Bringing the Sinners to Jesus," "Bring Them In," "Faith That Wins," "The Faith of the Soul-Winner."

The last title uses the key word from verse five. The body of the sermon will show the faith of the four men who brought the paralyzed sinner to Jesus. Study the passage again from this viewpoint. What does the passage say about the four men and their faith? The larger context (1:21–37) tells of Jesus' previous visit to the town. Many were healed of diseases and demons. "The whole town gathered at the door" (1:33). The four were probably in that crowd. They had heard Jesus, seen His miracles, and come to believe in Him. Use your imagination and see their cooperation, determination, and faith in action. They persevered against obstructions to get their friend to Jesus. It is an exciting picture of faith in action. Jesus "saw their faith," and they were blessed with the sight of their friend changed. The one they carried walked out the front door and carried his mat! The text offers these four points about the faith of the soul-winner:

    I. The soul-winner knows Jesus (1:21–37).
    II. The soul-winner believes Jesus can change anyone (2:3).
    III. The soul-winner has a determined faith (2:4).
    IV. The soul-winner's faith is not disappointed (2:5–12).

In each of these three sermons, the text and the specific objective controls the divisions. The body of the sermon develops in relationship to the specific objective. Only ideas that support the theme and specific objective are used in the body of the sermon. Would this idea fit in the above consecrative sermon: "Jesus has authority to forgive sins"? Verses 7–9 include this idea, but it doesn't fit the sermon on witnessing except as supporting material under division I. You could contrast what Jesus can do with what the religious leaders were doing. The idea is included in division III of the evangelistic sermon.

The major divisions of the sermon include explanation, illustration, and application of the idea to the listener. The body of the sermon also needs smooth movement between the major divisions. This movement can be accomplished by transition sentences.

TRANSITION SENTENCES

A transition sentence works like a door between one room and another. It connects the parts of the sermon and helps the unity of the sermon by relating one part to the other. Without transition sentences the sermon structure becomes like a disjointed skeleton. Transition sentences are usually of three types.[2]

1. Each division stated. This transition sentence states the previous concept and the one that follows. In the above sermon on Mark 2, the transition between the first and second division could be stated: "The soul-winner knows Jesus and also believes Jesus can change anyone." Both divisions are fully stated.
2. One division stated, the other suggested. This type of transition only states one of the two divisions. The transition between part two and three in the soul-winning sermon might read: (a) "The soul winner's faith believes Jesus changes anyone, but there is another quality to his faith." (b) "This is the second quality of the soul-winner's faith, but he also has a persevering faith." Sentence "a" states division II and suggests III. Sentence "b" suggests division II and fully states division III. Either kind of sentence may be used as a transition between the sermon divisions.
3. Both divisions suggested. In this transition neither division is fully stated. An example of this transition might be placed between division III and IV in the soul-winner's sermon of Mark 2, "These four men have shown us three qualities of their faith; there is one more quality."

The evangelistic sermon outline on Mark 2:1–12 is now expanded with the use of all these types of transitions. The transition sentences are italicized.

Overcoming the Paralysis of Sin

Introduction: It is possible to overcome the paralysis of sin, and here is the record of a man to whom it happened. If you desire it, you will have to do what he did.

I. You must acknowledge sin's paralysis (vv. 3–4). Are you willing to accept the fact you are helpless? Sin has paralyzed you. (This section explains the destructiveness of sin, man's helplessness to overcome it without conviction of the Spirit and repentance toward God.) *Overcoming sin begins when you acknowledge your condition and also when you receive the help of those who want you to overcome.*

II. Others do want you to overcome (vv. 3–5). How fortunate this paralytic was to have these four friends. They told him about Jesus; they carried him to Jesus. They overcame obstacles to get him before Jesus. They really wanted him to be changed. Others want you to overcome. Friends are praying; someone invited you here; your wife witnessed to you; a child gave you a Bible. How will you respond to this love? Listen to these loving friends who know Jesus, and you'll find it's true. *This paralyzed man has shown us two steps in overcoming sin, but there is another.*

III. Jesus has power to overcome your sin's paralysis (vv. 5–11). Everything else you've tried hasn't worked. Jesus can do it! His enemies said, "Who can forgive sin but God alone?" Jesus is God; He died for your sins. He arose from the grave victorious over sin and Satan. Jesus wants to say to everyone here today, "Son, your sins are forgiven!" *Jesus has power to overcome sin, but you must take one final step to experience the victory.*

IV. You will overcome sin when you trust and obey Jesus (v. 12). The man believed Jesus. "He got up, took up his mat and walked out in full view of them all." He heard Jesus and believed His word. Will you believe Jesus? If you really want to be free from sin's paralyzing power, you will trust Him now. He has the power to change your life. The Holy Spirit convicts you of the need to change. You must let Him do it. Others want you to trust Jesus, but it must be your decision. Decide now and know the victory of overcoming the paralysis of sin and the walk of a new life.

Transition sentences make a smooth transition between the sections of a sermon. Include some type of transition between the introduction and the first division and between each major division.

The body of the sermon develops one theme chosen from the text. The divisions are those which naturally come from the text. Omit material that does not support the main idea. Be sure each division supports the specific objective and connect each part of the sermon with transition sentences.

REACTION AND RESPONSE

Evaluate the sermon by Robert Russell, "If a Man Dies, Will He Live Again?" *Proclaim* 28, no. 4 (1999): 8–11.

Chapter 13
Sermon Structure

John A. Broadus compared the preacher to an architect. "Out of gathered materials he is to build a structure."[1] The sermon structure is the way the materials are arranged to present an understandable message. Confusion takes over without any structure, and "God is not the author of confusion" (1 Cor. 14:33). Paul's guideline for worship appropriately applies to preaching. "Let all things be done decently and in order" (1 Cor. 14:40). Sermon structure orderly arranges the materials to produce better communication.

What is the value of sermon structure? What advantages are there for a sermon to be organized? Structure makes the message understandable. Do you understand the arrangement of these letters—naerog? With a different arrangement they communicate—orange. The mind now visualizes an excellent fruit. If you ask a grocery attendant for a naerog, she will likely ask you to translate. Ask for an orange, and communication occurs. Surely you desire to be understood when you preach. Develop the arrangement of materials that will make your message better understood.

Structure makes the message more convincing. Preaching has the purpose of leading people to decision. You desire the hearers to "positively respond to the will of God." You can arrange the sermon materials in ways to make God's will more convincing. Sermon structure unites the materials around a central idea, like cutting down a tree with an axe. The lumberman does not hit at points up and down the tree. He cuts at one point until the tree falls. His entire body is coordinated and his energy turned to that one point. As W. E. Sangster noted, "No sermon is really strong which is not strong in structure too."[2]

Structure helps keep the listener's attention. The instruments of a band make different sounds. If each player sounded his own notes without any order, the listeners would quickly turn away. The sound would be unpleasant and uninteresting. When all the instruments play a piece of music with parts arranged, the result pleases the ear. People listen to know the entire arrangement. Most people who hear a band or orchestra do not know how the parts are arranged, but they like the result. The band keeps their attention. You can arrange the sermon to keep the listener's attention.

Structure helps people remember the message. Manuel Scott said every sermon should be "portable"; people ought to be able to take the message home with them.[3] The biblical truth and its application should become part of the listener's life. This isn't possible if they can't remember it. Sermon structure encourages the memory.

QUALITIES OF A GOOD SERMON STRUCTURE

A good sermon structure has four qualities: unity, natural arrangement, balance, and appeal. Unity means the arrangement supports a central idea. This idea comes from the text and is supported by each part of the sermon. Clovis Chappell said a sermon "ought to start, travel, and arrive."[4] Structure enables it to do this. Sometimes a preacher travels over many side roads before he reaches the destination. These detours detract from the central idea, make the sermon longer, and weaken the message.

This expository, doctrinal sermon outline on the Holy Spirit has unity in the arrangement.

The Spirit of God (John 3:8 KJV)
I. "The wind bloweth," the ceaseless action of the Spirit.
II. "where it listest," the sovereign freedom of the Spirit.
III. "and thou hearest the sound thereof," the indisputable evidence of the Spirit.
IV. "but canst not tell whence it cometh," the inscrutable origin of the Spirit.
V. "And whither it goeth," the incalcuable destiny of the Spirit.[5]

The arrangement of materials should be natural for the text or subject presented. The above sermon follows the words of the text. An evangelistc sermon on John 3 follows a natural outline from the text.

The Answer to Life's Supreme Search (John 3:1–15)
I. A man searches for life (vv. 1–2).
   Successful but unsatisfied; religious but uncertain.

II. Jesus supplies the answer to life's search (vv. 3–9).
You must be born again. The need for everyone (v. 3). The answer often misunderstood (v. 4). The search ends in a spiritual birth (vv. 5–8).
III. We must accept Jesus' answer to have life (vv. 9–15).
Accept Christ instead of religion (vv. 10–11). Believe Him, trust Him (vv. 12–15).

A large block of ice will not go through a funnel. The shape is unnatural for the container. Melt the ice and the water can be easily poured through the funnel. Do not force your sermon into an arrangement unnatural for the text. A natural arrangement moves toward a climax; the structure builds from the foundation to the completed structure.

A good sermon structure has balance. An automobile with one flat tire can be moved, but very slowly. The parts of a sermon should be balanced, with each section equally supported in relation to the central idea. This does not mean each part must have the same arrangement, as this student sermon indicates.

Living above the Ordinary (Daniel 1–3)

Daniel and his friends demonstrate a life above the ordinary.
I. Life above the ordinary has a high-standard lifestyle.
  A. Daniel and his friends chose this lifestyle (1:8).
  B. This lifestyle has high goals (1:4, 17–20).
  C. God's grace and mercy are needed to live this life (1:9,17; 2:28).
II. Life above the ordinary is life without compromise.
  A. Even when the majority compromises (3:7).
  B. Even when it means losing position.
  C. Even in the face of death.
  D. Even with or without God's deliverance (3:17–18).

The two parts contain different amounts of material. Yet the text supports all these ideas, and the sermon has balance.

Unbalanced sermon structure occurs when too much material is given to issues that are not important to the central idea. This additional material can take support away from the idea. Inadequate material on a major division also creates an unbalanced presentation.

Another quality of good sermon structure is appeal. Which captures the attention more, a brick or a flame? Certainly a flame has more appeal, for it is active, alive. Arrange your sermon materials to appeal to the hearers. A living body and a dead body both possess a skeleton. The skeleton gives structure, but without the life of the body it is useless, except to make it easier to remove the corpse. Your sermon structure needs a living quality that will appeal. Andrew W. Blackwood wrote, "Just as bones without flesh make a skeleton, so flesh without bones make a jellyfish. And neither bony skeletons nor jellyfish make good sermons."[6]

VARIETY IN SERMON STRUCTURE

Seek the best arrangement of materials and develop variety in the way you construct sermons. If you have the habit of constantly using the same arrangement, the people will show less interest. There are many varieties for sermon structure.

One arrangement groups material around the time something happened or should happen. A sermon on salvation can be arranged this way: We were saved (past—conversion); we are being saved (present—Christ is changing us now); we will be saved (future—when we get to heaven).

A sermon on a Bible personality can be arranged around events at different times in the person's life. Genesis 37–50 tells the story of Joseph. A sermon tracing God's providential work in Joseph's life would be developed around key scenes from Joseph's experience.

Another arrangement states a decision and then the results of that decision. An interesting sermon outline, "Supposing You Met Jesus," (Luke 24:33–35) used this approach.[7]

 I. You would reject sin and know forgiveness.
 II. You would want things put right with others.
 III. You would believe in yourself.
 IV. You would do His will.

A popular structure uses questions for the points of the sermon. John 3:1–17 was developed in this way: Who needs the new birth? What is the new birth? How is one born again? An interesting variety of this structure states the sermon divisions as answers to imagined questions: Sin requires the new birth (Why?); The Holy Spirit performs the new birth (How?); Everyone can be born again (Who?).

In the comparison-contrast sermon structure, two persons or truths are compared to show similarities or contrasted to show differences. Luke 16:19–31 can be arranged to show the contrast between the rich man and Lazarus. The result will show the advantages of Lazarus' faith.

Acts 14:8–18 was used in a sermon to preachers. It had two parts: preachers are men like others; preachers, are men unlike others. The sermon compared preachers to all men and then contrasted them. The first part stressed the humanity of preachers while the second part stressed the preacher's unique calling as a minister.

Many subjects can be developed with comparison-contrast, such as law and grace, the old and new covenants, faith or works, flesh and Spirit.

A problem to solution development introduces a problem and then offers a solution. It is frequently used in ethical sermons and also offers a good structure for pastoral sermons. "Turning Adversity into a Victory" (2 Chron. 32:1–8) presents the problem of suffering believers. Why do the faithful suffer? The message has two parts: the presence of adversity; coping with adversity. The first part presented the problem and gave some reasons why believers suffer. The second part showed some ways to respond to adversity.

Many sermons can be structured with only one major division. The body of the message explains, illustrates, and applies the one idea. The sermon might show how the idea works in a Bible personality, a person in history, and in the preacher's life. The sermon flows like a river, but the "river" stays within the channel of one theme.

INDUCTIVE/DEDUCTIVE PREACHING

Fred Craddock observed, "The method is the message. So is it with preaching: *how* one preaches is to a large extent *what* one preaches. It is not just the destination but the trip that is important."[8] Traditionally, most sermons travel a deductive road. The preacher states a thesis, explains and illustrates it, and then makes an application to specific needs. The deductive approach will continue to be a viable tool for communicating God's truth. This text emphasizes this approach as a beginning, but after developing basic study skills, a preacher should work on variety in form.

Why not develop a sermon inductively? Inductive preaching involves the congregation in the exciting discovery you experienced in the Inductive Bible Study. Instead of beginning with a proposition of truth found from the text and then proving it, begin with a need and allow the people to travel with you to the concluding truth.

Inductive preaching makes use of narrative. A story powerfully communicates truth. Scan through one of the Gospels and note the number of narrative descriptions of encounters with Jesus preserved by the Holy Spirit.

The congregation can be more involved by the use of questions. Include some of the questions you asked in the IBS. Direct and rhetorical questions

Sermon Structure

allow the listener to mentally respond to the message. Parable, analogy, and dialogue are other creative inductive techniques. Ralph L. Lewis wrote, "A sermon can be factually correct, homiletically sound, biblically accurate, doctrinally orthodox and still achieve nothing because it fails to involve the listeners. Involvement is the key. And listener involvement is the strength of the inductive process in preaching."9

TOPICAL OR EXPOSITORY

I've heard many sermons over the years and have noticed preachers favor topical messages. A topical sermon takes a subject and develops it apart from a primary text. The following doctrinal message on baptism is a topical sermon.

Why Do We Baptize?
  I. We baptize because of Jesus' example (Matt. 3:13–17).
  II. We baptize because of Jesus' command (Matt. 28:18–19).
  III. We baptize because of the New Testament pattern (Acts 2:40–41).
  IV. We baptize because of what baptism means (Rom. 6:3–4).

Each division in the sermon relates to the subject of baptism and answers the question asked in the title. The preacher created his own arrangement of materials based on relevant materials.

There are two common weaknesses of topical sermons. One weakness is making the topic too broad. A sermon on "The Resurrection of Jesus" tackled enough material for several sermons: the nature, the proof, the necessity, the results of Jesus' resurrection. The approach sounds more like a lecture than a living word. A topic without limits makes the sermon longer and more difficult to follow. A second failure of many topical sermons is a weak connection to Scripture. "He took his text from the Scripture and departed therefrom, never to return again," is an often repeated description of this weakness. A truly biblical sermon must have the idea solidly based on Scripture.

An expository sermon takes a passage of Scripture and "exposes" the meaning and applies it to life. The subject and the body of the message come from the text. An expository sermon usually contains more Scripture teaching and results in more systematic study of the Bible.

"Expository sermons are monotonous and boring" is an oft-repeated objection to this style of preaching. Such an objection is fed by the example of a preacher who only "reads a passage and makes a running comment on them," usually unrelated to the needs of the people.

Expository sermons often suffer from a lack of unity. The sermon becomes a series of thoughts on each verse; the result seems like unstrung pearls. Which of these two approaches to 2 Peter 1:1–11 is stronger?

2 Peter 1:1–11
In the beginning of his second letter, Peter gives us many truths.
1. He reminds us of his authority (v. 1).
2. He writes to the saved. We have been put right with God. Our faith is as precious as Peter's.
3. Two blessings are ours: grace and peace (v. 2).
4. Christ gives us all we need (v. 3).
5. We must add to our faith (vv. 5–9). These additions will make us effective.
6. Are you sure about your calling? (v. 10).
7. Will you be welcomed in heaven? (v. 11).

The Blessings of Knowing Jesus (2 Peter 1:1–11)

Three times in this passage Peter writes about the "knowledge of our Lord Jesus Christ" (vv. 2, 3, 8). These verses tell us some blessings we have because we know the Lord Jesus.
1. We have the blessing of equal standing before Him (v. 1). Peter is a great servant and apostle but our faith is as precious as his. Each Christian receives grace and peace.
2. We have the blessing of abundant life (vv. 3–7).
3. We can have the blessing of an effective and fruitful service (vv. 8–9).
4. We will have the eternal blessing when we are welcomed into heaven (v. 11)!

All of these blessings come as a result of knowing the Lord Jesus.

John Broadus offered several suggestions for preparing better expository sermons.[10] Carefully choose from the text the details you will emphasize. Use only the most important details and those which support the main theme of the message. Avoid quoting too many references from other parts of the Bible; this will lessen attention on the text. Finally, be sure the exposition applies to life. It is not enough to explain Scripture; people need help for living.

Structure makes a message understandable and more convincing. The form of the message helps the listener's attention and retention of the message. A good structure will have unity, natural arrangement, balance, and appeal. There are an endless variety of ways to structure a message. Fred

Craddock reminds us, "He who trumpets "Reveille" *every* Sunday should not be surprised that the congregation ceases to believe a new day dawns; he who sounds "Taps" every week should realize the listeners do not really believe the curtain of life has fallen."[11]

REACTION AND RESPONSE

Another approach to sermon structure uses a probing question and a unifying word. Study this approach in Harold T. Bryson, and James C. Taylor, *Building Sermons to Meet People's Needs* (Nashville: Broadman Press, 1980), 81–102. Use this approach and develop a structure for your message on Luke 14:25–27.

Chapter 14
"In Conclusion"

Eutychus went to sleep during Paul's sermon and fell from the window (Acts 20:9–12). While the apostle "talked on and on," Eutychus might have wondered if Paul knew how to conclude a sermon! You need to know some ways to conclude your message.

The sermon conclusion brings the sermon to an appropriate end. It is your last opportunity to relate the Scripture to life. In the conclusion, the listeners are faced with decisions to make as a result of the message. Though it seems to be a logical way to close a sermon, it is not the best way. To simply stop your message after the last division is unnatural and ineffective.

In a court trial, the lawyer's conclusion is very important. He works hard on this final appeal to the judge and jury. The final opportunity has arrived to convince the judge or jury of the rightness of his side. Broadus believed the conclusion is more important than the introduction.

I titled this section "In Conclusion," to make you aware of this often used way of beginning the closing section of the message. It isn't very effective because it diverts your listeners' attention from the message to concerns of leaving the service. They also may have different expectations of the length it takes to conclude and become wary if you don't "wrap it up right away." Some have described an optimist as someone who reaches for his hat when the preacher says, "And finally brethren." As illustrations do not need explaining, neither does the conclusion need to be identified as such. Also, stay away from the use of "finally," and "as we close." Everyone will know you have reached the conclusion when you stop!

AN EFFECTIVE CONCLUSION

An effective conclusion has unity with the body of the sermon. The conclusion logically follows the introduction and body of the sermon. It makes no sense apart from the material which went before it. As a vital part of the sermon, do not treat the conclusion as an addition. It must be closely connected to the body of the message. The conclusion supports the text and the purpose of the message.

Unity with the body of the sermon is preserved when no new ideas are added to the conclusion. The conclusion ends what the introduction presents and the body expands. The conclusion serves and supports the message; it does not present a new message.

A sermon entitled, "An Invitation Especially for You," presented four invitations issued by the Lord. The four parts of the sermon are expressed in the conclusion as questions. The conclusion did not consider any material unrelated to these ideas.

> Which invitation do you need to accept? Surely one is especially for you! Has God been calling for your life? Offer it in His service. Do you need to rededicate your life? Surrender yourself completely to Christ. Should your membership be in this church? You need a church home! Why waste a week of Christian service? Come now! Are you lost in sin? Are you away from Christ? Trust Jesus Christ as your Savior. Come right now. Say, "Lord, I believe you. I trust you."
>
> I invite you to come, the pastor invites you to come, this church is eager for you to come. The Lord loves you and wants you to be a part of this church. He invites you to come. Come for all things are now ready. Come as we sing.[1]

This conclusion is united with the body of the sermon. It concludes the subject introduced in the beginning and explained in the body. No new ideas are put forth in the conclusion.

In a sermon, "Future Glory and Rewards," a student presented two points—our future glory with Christ and the rewards (crowns) we will receive. The message concluded:

> Do you want the crown? Jesus was able to endure the cross by setting his eye on the goal ahead. We who know Him as Savior and Lord are able to endure temptation as we fix our eyes on the future rewards.

The crowns just mentioned are ones that believers can receive. Even the word "crown" is a reminder to us of the crown of thorns worn by Jesus when He went to the cross to pay the penalty for our sins. John 19:5—a mock coronation when they crowned the Lord Jesus with a crown of thorns. What a demonstration of the depravity of fallen man. He bore the curse so we would not be cursed.

The specific objective aimed the sermon at Christians, not unbelievers. It was about rewards not the curse. The preacher diverted the key word "crown" to a different idea during the conclusion. Present no new ideas in the conclusion. The conclusion must have unity with the body of the sermon.

An effective conclusion is personal. Think of the listeners when you conclude. Speak directly to them in a warm, personal way. Using personal pronouns will help do the job: you, yours, we, us, ours, I. Read again the conclusion to the message about the four invitations found earlier in this chapter. Circle the personal pronouns. Notice the personal nature of that conclusion.

Express your pastor's heart when you conclude the message. Apply the truth of the message to the local situation. A. J. Gossip delivered one of history's outstanding sermons immediately after his wife's death. The entire sermon is very personal. The close relationship between pastor and people added to the power of the message. The message, "But When Life Tumbles In, What Then?" concludes:

> I don't think you need be afraid of life. Our hearts are very frail; and there are places where the road is very steep and very lonely. But we have a wonderful God. And as Paul puts it, what can separate us from His love? Not death, he says immediately, pushing that aside at once as the most obvious of all possibilities.
>
> No, not death. For, standing in the roaring of the Jordan, cold to the heart with its dreadful chill, and very conscious of the terror of its rushing, I too, like Hopeful, can call back to you who in your turn will have to cross it, "Be of good cheer, my brother, for I feel the bottom, and it is sound."[2]

Notice this conclusion deals only with the subject introduced in the sermon—God's victory in life's difficulties, especially death. It has unity with the body of the sermon. It is personal. Ten personal pronouns are found in these two short paragraphs. Be personal in your conclusion.

Conclude your message with a dynamic sense of urgency. Plead with compassion and conviction. Speak with assurance and challenge. Broadus wrote of the sermon which concludes like "the emptying of a pitcher with a few drops and dregs."[3] Stay away from that kind of conclusion!

An urgent and dynamic conclusion is not measured by the loudness of the voice. The quiet voice can also be very effective. Evangelist Billy Graham concludes with urgency, often sounding like a counselor. One of his sermons, "The Fruit of the Spirit," has this conclusion:

> As you yield completely to Him as Savior and Lord and when you come to Christ by an act of faith, He gives you the Holy Spirit who produces the fruit of the Spirit. . . .
>
> You say, what do you want me to do? I believe in God, I believe in Christ, I believe the Bible, isn't that enough? No! By an act of faith you must receive Christ. You must give Him your total life, your intellect, your emotional life. Your will must be bent to His will—surrender, commit, receive. "But as many as received Him to them gave He power to become the sons of God, even to them that believe on His name" (John 1:12). Give your life to Him! Don't let anything keep you back! You may never be this close to the kingdom of God again.[4]

Joshua concluded his message to Israel with an urgent, personal appeal. "Choose for yourselves this day whom you will serve. . . . But as for me and my household, we will serve the Lord" (Josh. 24:15).

The conclusion should be specific, prepared with the specific objective in mind. Clearly direct the conclusion to the target audience. Clearly say what you want them to do.

Abstract, general ideas do not belong in the conclusion. Make specific applications. Leave no doubt about what you want the people to do. The Billy Graham sermon, noted above, was preached in an evangelistic crusade. His objective was to see lost people trust Jesus Christ as Lord. The sermon showed that only those who are born again can produce the fruit of the Spirit. A person still under the control of the flesh remains a slave to sin. His conclusion asked for people to trust Christ. He called for an "act of faith. . . . Give your life to Him."

Look back again at the first sample conclusion in this chapter—"An Invitation Especially For You." The preacher asks for four decisions. He appeals to four different groups of people in the congregation who need to make decisions. He is specific in what they are asked to do. His invitation would need to devote separate appeals to each group.

The conclusion of a sermon on Romans 12:1–2 went like this:

> After finding out and understanding what comprises a life worth living for Christ, is your heart still divided? Is your "boat" sinking now? Do you have so many things in your life still dividing your attention to Him? Are you living a surrendered life? A holy life? A transformed life? Or are you still conforming to this passing world? We should live for Him and serve Him fully and not half-heartedly. Are you living for Christ or for yourself?

This conclusion lacks specifics. Illustrate the divided life. The conclusion contains many unanswered questions. Positive, urgent appeal to take specific action would make a stronger conclusion. People may have heard all the good sounding church language but still wonder, "What do I do? What Now? So What?"

VARIETY IN CONCLUSION

There are different ways to conclude the message. Successful preachers use several ways. A frequently used way to conclude is to summarize the major divisions. This does not mean just repeating them as I, II, III. They can be restated with a slight change of words. Their connection with the text can be reemphasized. This sermon conclusion shows an effective summary of the major divisions.

How the New Testament Punctuates the Gospel[5] (Matt. 11:2–11; Phil. 4:4–7)

> And there I leave it. It's the drama of human life in the grip of the Eternal God. "Art thou He?" "The Lord is at hand." "Rejoice in the Lord!" From a question mark to a period to an exclamation point. So does the New Testament punctuate the gospel. You'll not get them all neatly arranged like that, each one treading on the other's heels. They'll be jostling one another, slipping in and out of the hymns you sing, interrupting the Lord's Prayer. But that's what faith means. What else could it mean, when you come to think of it, with lives like ours, and such a God as this?

This conclusion also uses the sermon title. The entire sermon is briefly summarized in these few closing comments. When using this type of conclusion, be careful that you do not "re-preach" the message.

Another way to conclude is with additional application. Show what effect the truth of the message will have on the hearers. Relate the idea of the message to an opportunity, a duty, or a challenge. Of course, you will have application throughout the message. The conclusion can also apply the subject to the hearer's life.

The conclusion of a stewardship sermon based on Exodus 35:20–29 refers to a later passage to show the results of giving. The sermon title was "From Heart to Hand."

> Exodus 36:5 reveals the marvelous results of hearts stirred by love and possessed with a willing spirit. "The people bring much more than enough for the service of the work which the Lord commanded us to do." Here is the way to reach our church budget. Here is the key to unlock the resources we need. Love and a willing heart. The issue is personal. Do we love? Are we willing? Our heart moves our hand. Oh God, change my heart that my hands will give what is needed to do your work.

A third type of conclusion restates the text. This approach proves effective when a shorter text is used. Application can be inserted between the words of the text, as this sermon did.

> Jesus our leader is completely honest when He calls us—Follow Me, I will make you fishers of men. Follow Me! No other leader is worthy nor capable. Place your complete loyalty in Him. Follow me. Obedience is our response. Consistent following of the Master will achieve so much more. And we have the blessed assurance that in following "He will make us." He isn't finished yet. Our desires to be a fervent witness or anything else in His service can become real. Only when we follow. Only when we submit ourselves into His hands.

Conclude by a repetition of the theme. Using 2 Corinthians 12:1–7 as a text, a sermon included this theme sentence in the introduction: "With God's help he gained strength out of his weaknesses." In the conclusion these sentences restated the theme. "The weaknesses of life do not have to make us weaker. By God's help we may gain strength during times of weaknesses."[6]

A story can be used to conclude the sermon. Be sure it throws light on the theme and motivates the listeners to action. "Turning Adversity into a Victory" was concluded with an experience from the life of Helen Keller.

> Helen Keller spoke and everyone present was deeply moved by the message of the famous blind woman. In a question and answer period which followed, a university student asked, "Ms. Keller, what would you rather have

than anything in all the world?" The audience expected her to say, "My eyes and ears so that I can see and hear." Instead she responded, "What would I rather have than anything in all the world? I'll tell you. World peace and brotherhood and that all men will know Jesus Christ as I know him." There was silence and then the people broke into cheers. Many threw their hats into the air; it was a rare and electrifying moment. Helen Keller lost much, but through her adversity she had discovered the most important. To know Jesus is to have power and a Person who makes it possible to face blindness or any adversity that comes and turn that adversity into a victory.

Poetry or words of music are another option for concluding the sermon. Carefully choose the selection so that it will strongly support the theme. It might be popular or beautiful and your favorite, but it must be appropriate to the text and to conclude the entire message. The effectiveness of poetry and music words depends much on the delivery. Emphasize key words. Appropriate pauses and voice tone make the presentation more meaningful.

In the following conclusion a poem is used to close. Notice no comment is made about the poem; this would detract from its effectiveness.

> I should be a fool to stand here today and talk to you about religion, if I were not dead sure of that elemental fact. I know whom I have believed. I know that His promise stands fast forever.
>
> Jesus, my Lord! I know His Name,
> His Name is all my boast;
> Nor will He put my soul to shame,
> Nor let my hope be lost.
> I know that safe with Him remains,
> Protected by His power,
> What I've committed to His trust,
> Till the decisive hour.[7]

THE INVITATION

My church experience has always been for the conclusion of the message to lead into an invitation for public commitment. Some churches win many to Christ and grow their membership without a public invitation and response. The practice of an invitation certainly has biblical support (Ex. 32:26; Josh. 24:15; Isa. 55:1; Rev. 22:17). Jesus frequently said, "Come." He publicly invited His disciples to follow Him. An invitation naturally flows from the good news of Jesus. Specific and public responses affirm personal growth as the individual's responsibility is stressed. Individuals who make public decisions feel the prayer support of the church, and others are encouraged to "bear one another's burdens."

When you issue an invitation, treat it seriously and trust the Lord for guidance. Pray for His direction for He changes lives. Invite people to Him and depend on the power of the Holy Spirit to convince people, according to the promise of Scripture (John 16:8).

Allow time for the Holy Spirit to do His work. If people do not respond in a reasonable time, then close the invitation. A long invitation without response appears to be pressure from the preacher. Decisions made from pressure often prove false. Allow each person to make his own decision. If people resist, respect their freedom and will to decide. They may never come back if you embarrass them.

Issue the invitation with confidence and positive expectation, a good approach for the entire message. Expect people to respond; speak to encourage their response. God is "pleading through us" (2 Cor. 5:20). Confidence and expectation did not inspire these invitation comments:

> "Is there anyone here who wants to be saved?"
> "I don't know if you need to come, but we're going to have an invitation."
> "We're going to sing this verse; if no one comes the service is over."
> "Maybe you feel like making a decision."

Confident expectation would include these comments:

> "Who will be the first to decide?"
> "You came today with this decision on your mind. Don't wait any longer to trust Christ."
> "Jesus said, 'All things are ready.' You are ready also. Come now."
> "There is a father here struggling with God's will. God knows you and loves you. The Lord waits now to receive you, dad."

If you are the pastor, be fully involved in the invitation. Be at the front to counsel those who decide. Prepare other members to provide counsel when several decisions are made. Prolonged counseling of an individual by the pastor may discourage others from coming. The pastor should never direct the invitation song. You need to be free to assist those who make decisions. Be alert to the congregation instead of having your attention in the hymnbook.

The content of the invitation depends on the specific objective. The specific objective focuses on the target audience and what you want them to do.

In the invitation, speak to these and ask them to do what your objective states. An evangelistic sermon targeted for the lost should have an invitation asking the unsaved to turn from sin and trust Christ. A sermon on baptism with an objective for "unbaptized believers to obey Christ and be baptized," should have an invitation with an appeal such as, "You were converted one year ago but still not baptized. Obey Christ; come now and follow Him in baptism." A consecrative sermon on witnessing has this objective, "Christians committed to regular witnessing." The invitation will invite believers to commit themselves to "talk to at least one lost person each week." Ask the people to make a specific decision. Leave no doubt as to what you want them to do.

You should first invite people to make decisions related to your sermon. After time for these decisions, ask for other decisions.

You might be asking, "How do I move from the sermon into the invitation?" This needs to be a natural transition, smooth without seeming staged. You can ask for the people to bow their heads and consider God's invitation. Explain the decisions; pray for them. A song can then be sung while you wait for people to decide. Clearly state what you want them to do before you ask them to stand. After part of the song, you can plead again for decisions. Follow Peter's example: "with many other words he warned them; and he pleaded with them" (Acts 2:40).

Clothe the entire invitation in a positive spirit. Rejoice in the Lord! Wait upon the Spirit. He has done His work even when you do not see outward decisions. Trust God's promise for His word:

> It shall not return to me void, but it will accomplish what I please and it shall prosper in the thing for which I sent it. (Isaiah 55:11)

REACTION AND RESPONSE

Evaluate the following conclusion. Does it include the characteristics of an effective conclusion? The student message used Paul's life as an example of God's providence in the life of Christian workers.

> Yes, from the beginning of our ministry until we have completed our task, God's providence can be clearly seen. Oh, how great and awesome is God's providence for us! He guides all things for good. May the daily ministry problems and the dangers and risks we face cause us not to be afraid or lose heart.

"In Conclusion"

There was a journeyman who wished to travel around the world in a homemade boat. On the day he launched into the ocean, people watching shouted, "You'll never make it," "You'll run out of food!" But a friend approached and shouted—"You'll make it! Bon Voyage!" By the way, he made it, and his name is now in the Guinness Book of World Records.

The ministry is like a journey. There are problems, dangers, great risks and discouragements along the way. But we have a friend, the God whom we serve. He tells us to continue and finish the task entrusted to us. Trust Him and submit to Him your life, your problems, your future. His providence demands our complete submission to His will. Fellow workers, bon voyage!

Chapter 15
Introduction, Please

"Age is an unkind thief. It steals without conscience or remorse, taking only what is most precious."[1] Thus a sportswriter began an article on legendary golfer Ben Hogan, who had to give up golf because of age. Surely a preacher can introduce his subject in as interesting a manner as a sportswriter. My fifteen-year-old daughter suggested, "Start with something that catches your attention; that will make you want to listen."

Prepare the introduction after interpreting the text and developing the body of the message. By then you will know the subject, and a stronger introduction is more likely.

The introduction has three main purposes. It should, first of all, secure the attention of the listeners. One famous preacher said, "There is no room for debate as to what the introduction ought to do. We are simply trying to get our people to want to hear what we have to say."[2] Loss of attention at the beginning makes it very difficult to get it later in the sermon. The congregation should immediately share your feelings about the significance of your subject. The introduction should encourage a desire to hear what you have to say.

Beyond securing attention, the introduction presents the sermon idea. The thesis sentence ought to be included in the introduction. With the beginning comments, the listeners will know the direction of the message. Presentation of the theme builds a foundation for all that follows. A good introduction makes it easier to understand the message.

The introduction also introduces the text. Remember you are preaching biblical sermons, and the idea comes from the text. Presenting the text in the introduction will add authority to the message, and you will show your desire to present a Bible message.

A MORE EFFECTIVE INTRODUCTION

Awareness of some basics will help you develop a better beginning for your sermons. Make the beginning truly an introduction to the message. Introduce the theme but omit parts of the body. You might find the letters TTT a helpful reminder. The introduction usually contains the thesis, text, and title. These three elements are good ways to introduce the subject and show the direction of the message. Use interesting material but refrain from talking about anything unrelated to your subject.

A good sermon can be undone by beginning with an apology. Some apologetic comments I've heard preachers make are:

I'm not sure I understand the meaning of this text.

I didn't sleep well last night, so the sermon may not be too good.

You've heard better sermons on this passage, but the Lord wants me to preach on it anyway.

I didn't get to study as much as I wanted this week, our baby was sick.

These kinds of comments put attention on the wrong things. The introduction tries to interest the listeners; apologies add doubts to the listeners' minds and cause them to look for weaknesses in the message. Instead of showing humility, apologies show a lack of trust in the Lord to overcome a problem. The people will certainly know if your message is weak! Don't apologize in the introduction.

Interesting language in the first few sentences can hook people's attention. A sermon on Isaiah 53:1, "Who has believed our report? and to whom has the arm of the Lord been revealed?" began with this sentence: "One of life's most irritating experiences is that of talking to persons who are not listening."[3] These are some opening sentences in sermons about Bible personalities.

God is the only Master with servants who accepts the intention for the action (David).

The shipwreck of Solomon is surely the most terrible tragedy in all the world.

> Matthew loved money. Matthew, like Judas, must have money. With clean hands if he could; but clean hands or unclean, Matthew must have money.[4]

Use your imagination to create a more interesting introduction. A sermon about Abraham and Isaac had this introduction. "It was early in the morning, very early in the morning when he arose. He took his son and her son away from the tent. He must take him now before it is light, before she awakes."[5]

The introduction is another place for variety. Too many preachers get into the habit of beginning in the same way, such as, "In the brief time I have left I want to speak about," or "The title of today's sermon is . . . and the text is found in . . ."

The most common introduction begins with the text. You have probably heard sermons started like this, "God's message today is from Ephesians 6:18. Paul tells us to pray in the Spirit. Prayer is listed as a resource to fight against the Devil. The Scripture gives us two encouragements to keep on praying."

Does this beginning offer more appeal, interest, and secure attention any better?

> Battles are won the night before. If Satan can discourage us in prayer, he has already won the battle. An ineffective prayer life makes us an easy target for Satan. We enter spiritual battles weakened. We are not able to use our other spiritual resources. That's what Paul said, recorded in Ephesians 6:18. After describing other parts of the Christians battle gear, Paul tells us to "Keep On Praying." Keep on praying because the Devil tries to undermine our prayer life.

Beginning with the text gives authority to the message, but use variety in the way you introduce the text. Often you will include some background information from your Bible study which helps understand the text and your chosen theme.

In chapter 10 you learned how to study the context of a passage. Include some of the material from your context studies if it helps explain the text and support the theme. You can easily use too much time describing details of the historical setting. Don't get lost in description nor make people feel this is a history lesson without any application to them.

One of the best ways to secure attention and keep interest is to begin with current experience. Romans 5:1–5 was the text on the subject, "A Hope That Never Disappoints." I preached it once with an opening illustration focusing on my sister's "hope chest," into which she put items in hope of her future marriage. Some girls with hope chests have had their hopes disappointed. Our hope in Christ never disappoints, and Romans 5 tells us why. The opening caught the interest of older women, many of whom had grown up with "hope chests."

Later I preached the message with an introduction which included brief scenes from the lives of three people. A college student trying to cope with an unplanned pregnancy and a hastily advised abortion; a couple, married fifteen years, facing divorce because of the husband's adultery; a thirty-five-year old man dying with cancer. After each scene I asked, "Does the gospel offer them anything more? Do they have any hope?" The three points of the message focused on hope for sin, stress, and eternity. After the section on sin, I told how the college student found forgiveness and a new life. During the division on stress, I described how the couple overcame their fractured marriage and moved ahead with meaning. In the section on eternity, the people heard of the victorious death of the cancer patient and his family's hope for the future. I noticed a much higher interest span because of the current relevance with which I began and which I maintained throughout the message.

While living in the Philippines, we experienced a people's revolution and change of government. A popular slogan during those days of mass demonstrations was, "The voice of the people is the voice of God." Shortly after the government changed, I preached a sermon entitled, "Is the Voice of the People the Voice of God?" In the introduction I asked, "Who speaks for God? Is the voice of the people the voice of God?" The sermon answered that question, but the text was not used until later in the message. The first two points used other Scriptures to show the false idea in the popular saying. Hebrews 1, the primary text, stressed the positive—God speaks for Himself, He speaks through His word, and He speaks through Christ. The message would have been less interesting had I started with Hebrews. Starting with present-day experiences, I could tell from the pulpit I had their attention. Members invited me to preach that message to two other groups (one educational, the other professional) during the following month.

The present-day life experience can be a problem facing the congregation. The theme can be linked with a current need in the church or community. A seminary professor heard 119 preachers during a year traveling over America "searching for excellence in preaching."

> I found 24 percent (of the sermons) outstandingly interesting . . . The preachers of these excellent sermons were obviously aware of the needs of the people.

> The best sermons I heard were interesting to me because I sensed that they were also interesting to people around me. The preachers kept the attention of their people because the messages were specifically designed for their particular congregations. Pastors were communicating with their own people.[6]

Design the sermon introduction to interest the people who hear you preach. The above comments apply to the entire sermon also.

Many times you will preach on a special occasion. This event might be a church anniversary, church organization, ordination, mission emphasis, or school program. Interest and attention comes as you begin with reference to the occasion, significant persons, or events related to the occasion. A little investigation can often reveal an interesting historical illustration which ties in with the occasion. Your interest in the people helps secure their interest in your message. Determine if the program has a theme verse on which you can preach, unless the program already includes someone to do that.

The sermon can be introduced with some of the same approaches described in the chapter on conclusions. Begin with a quotation, a story, poetry, or words of music. In all cases the material chosen must be brief and interesting and truly help to introduce the theme. A sermon on 1 John 1:8–9 may be introduced in any of these ways. The subject is how a Christian overcomes sin. Different titles might be needed; the story supplies an interesting title. Which introduction interests you the most?

Observation

"Saints Refinished," that's what the sign said. I glanced back to be sure. A closer look revealed it to be a shop which specializes in refinishing religious statues. The offer it made is one every Christian needs. Not for our statues, but for ourselves. The Bible calls us saints, but we are certainly not perfect. There are times when we need refinishing. Here is the way: "If we confess our sin, He is faithful and just, and will forgive our sin and cleanse us from all unrighteousness." (1 John 1:8–9)

Poetry

Robert Browning wrote,

> Good to forget—
> Best to forgive!

Our God is best at what we occasionally achieve. He is the best forgiver. He is faithful and just to forgive our sins and cleanse us from all unrighteousness.

Quotation

"People think the confessional is unknown in Protestant churches. It is a great mistake. The principal change is that there is no screen between the penitent and the father confessor." Oliver Wendell Holmes is right. We have no screen between us and our confessor. Our God is our confessor. . . . He asks us to come to Him and 'confess our sins.' It is the first step toward forgiveness.

Words of Music

Like a river glorious	Perfect, yet it floweth
Is God's perfect peace,	Fuller everyday
Over all victorious	Perfect, yet it groweth
In its bright increase.	Deeper all the way.

Those words were written by one who sought the peace of a victorious Christian life. While studying 1 John 1:7–9 she saw "it as a flash of light." Her study revealed that the verb in verse 9 means "keeps on cleansing." She claimed Christ's promise of constant victory. What Frances Havergal discovered you can also have. Constant victory in Christ comes with our continual cleansing.

Life Experience

To look at the young college student, you would think she had everything going for her. She saw the future quite differently. An undisciplined relationship had resulted in a pregnancy. Her mother encouraged her to have an abortion and get on with her life. Now her life had met a dead end. She felt used, guilty, and unable to forgive herself. Do you think she needed 1 John 5:8–9?

You can readily see the same message can begin in many ways. Whichever way you use, you will usually soon include your thesis and text. Check the above introductions on how they included the thesis and text. Many times you can use the title in the introduction. Practice a variety of introductions, and it will make your preaching more interesting.

REACTION AND RESPONSE

Study the sermon, "A Case Study in Temptation," Haddon W. Robinson, *Biblical Sermons* (Grand Rapids: Baker, 1989), 15–22. Relate the introduction to concepts presented in this lesson. How does the introduction fit the particular audience where the message was preached? (see Robinson, 23).

Unit 5

Putting Light on the Truth

A friend of mine operates a home and commercial lighting firm in central Florida. An amazing variety of fixtures fills his showroom. No wonder he has a good business. He makes an effort to meet the varied needs and interests of customers. Fixtures are designed to apply light at different angles and intensity. Others are made to convey a mood or to blend with an architectural theme. Some will be purchased on the basis of cost or the size of the room in which they will be used. The entire business reflects creativity, public need, and a desire to serve others.

Application, illustration, and imagination throw light on the truth of your text and help the listeners see the relevance and need of your subject. These three key elements hold tremendous potential for securing and holding the interest of your listeners and motivating them to respond positively to the will of God.

You face your hardest work at the point of application, illustration, and imagination. And also the most subtle temptation. Many preachers work to understand a text and explain it and think they have done all that is needed. Often they never get out of the Bible into life. The truth of the text keeps circling the field, searching for a place to land and unload. The people may leave thinking, "He knows a lot about the Bible, but I wish he understood my problem." Work for contemporary application and illustration.

Does imagination belong in a text on biblical preaching? Maybe the question assumes a wrong definition of imagination. I don't mean mixing myth and falsehood with the truth to make it more palatable to twenty-first century hearers. I do mean using the mind our Lord gave each of us to creatively picture the events of Scripture. This light will help others see the truth needed for life.

Jesus, "the light of the world," came in a very creative display of God's power, illustrating the Father's love. In Him the Light and the Truth become one. We can only imagine what it will be like when we see Him in that city where He is the light.

Chapter 16
The Text and Life Application

In a day when 42 percent of our inactive church members dropped out of the church because of irrelevant sermons, we need to learn to apply the sermon to the lives of our people. This can and should be done throughout the message."[1] Brian L. Harbour demonstrated that a meaningful sermon applies the text to life. Specific examples of the scriptural truth are needed. In a sermon on prayer, James 1:6–7 was quoted, "ask in faith with no doubting." The text was applied to a life situation by using an illustration from a book. The sermon contained this section.

> Rosalind Rinker suggests you "ask only for that which you confidently believe He could do." She illustrates this by her daughter's concern for an unsaved friend. Her prayers for him began with a request for courage to talk with him. Then she prayed for his willing acceptance of a New Testament. Step by step she prayed in faith without doubting. Each time her prayers were followed by faith in action. Two weeks after her first request, the friend openly trusted Christ. Believing God can is not the same as believing God will.

The text was applied by a specific example of how to pray without doubting. The hearer has the feeling—"I can do that." Life application helps the sermon achieve its purpose.

BIFOCAL PREACHING

Some use a term which helps us remember the need for life application. They encourage "Bifocal Preaching." Bifocals enable the wearer to see things close as well as faraway. Preaching demands these two essentials. The preacher studies the Word of God to determine its meaning. He also looks at the needs of life. A proper interpretation of the text results in applying the truth of Scripture to life needs. When a sermon has much Bible material but does not relate it to life, the preacher is only looking through the top part of the glass. A sermon may have much material about life needs and be separated from Scripture. In this case the preacher is looking through only the bottom part. Bifocal preaching balances what the Bible means and what the Bible says to today's people. Bible interpretation and life application together make a strong sermon. "We should be praying that God will raise up a new generation of Christian communicators who struggle to relate God's unchanging Word to our ever-changing world."[2] A look in three directions encourages life application.

Look at the Present

You have already been encouraged to study the historical and social context of the Scripture. You must know what the Word said to those who first heard it. Beware of letting your sermon get lost in word study and background material and remain in the past. Look at the present. "In preaching, it is necessary to follow the direction of the text and relate it to our own time; the text shows where the road leads, but we have to walk on it at the present time."[3]

Jim Lowery wrote, "Effective biblical preaching brings together then and now."[4] Every word of the text should be studied to discover the meaning. Specific application to present situations must then be made. The Bible records historical events; it is also "living and active. Sharper than any double-edged sword, it penetrates . . . it judges the thoughts and attitudes of the heart" (Heb. 4:12). Application has done its work when the hearers experience the word piercing their heart and mind.

John 4 pictures Jesus as a man without prejudice toward women and other races. Sermons explain the Jewish attitude toward women and the Jewish-Samaritan prejudice. Some cite geography to illustrate how Jesus traveled the unfamiliar route to demonstrate His love for all people. Preachers state the truth "God loves all people." *Make the present-day application.* Racial and sexual prejudice remains a current problem. Men still treat women as objects for fleshly satisfaction or as inferior to men. Discrimination continues in housing, employment, and attitude. Use current examples to apply the truth of Jesus' example. Apply the truth with a story, an illustration, a life experience of your own or another, or ask probing questions.

Paul Scherer wrote, "Because Christianity is rooted in history, people think they can bury it there. And preachers sometimes help."[5] You help bury

The Text and Life Application

the message in the past by overusing the past tense. Use active present tense verbs when you preach. "Jesus is alive! He lavishes His love on all of us! He asks us to love blacks." Life application improves with present-day illustrations. Sermon illustrations from preachers of a former generation may be dated and irrelevant. Interest increases when people hear contemporary illustrations. Current illustrations of Bible truths demonstrate the relevance of the Bible for today's people. Stories you know, current publications, radio, television, movies, or music may give you present-day illustrations of biblical truths.

Look to the People

James Stewart suggested that during preparation of our sermon we "visualize a gathered congregation."[6] What needs of the church does the text address? What problems are the people now facing? Apply the text to people of different ages in the congregation. It was said of Halford Luccock, "He started his sermon and meditations at the sidewalk level with the problems people were facing, and then led them back into the biblical uplands to the springs of renewal and strength."[7]

A continuous look at congregation needs results in a more specific sermon. During preparation relate the idea of the text to the people who will hear it. Use the language of the average person and speak on the practical level. Personal pronouns—you, us, we, our—tie the text to the people.

Paul's sermon in Athens (Acts 17:22–31) reflects his awareness of the people. He had earlier seen "the city was full of idols." His experience became a current illustration for his message. Notice the personal pronouns and the quotation from one of their popular poets.

> Men of Athens! I see that in every way you are very religious. For as I walked around and observed your objects of worship, I even found an altar with this inscription: To An Unknown God. Now what you worship as something unknown I am going to proclaim to you.

> The God who made the world and everything in it is the Lord of heaven and earth and does not live in temples built by hand . . . as some of your poets have said, "We are his offspring."

The needs of the Athenian audience are seen in Paul's appeal. "Now (God) commands all people everywhere to repent. For he has set a day when he will judge the world by justice by the man he has appointed" (vv. 30–31). Local needs add urgency to the message.

The Old Testament prophet Malachi looked to the people in his preaching. He imagined questions which the people mentally asked as he preached.

> "I have loved you," says the Lord. But you ask, "How have you loved us?" (1:2)

> "You place defiled food on my altar." But you ask, "How have we defiled you?" (1:6–7)

> "Return to me, and I will return to you," says the Lord Almighty. But you ask, "How are we to return?" Will a man rob God? Yet you rob me. But you ask, "How do we rob you?" (3:7–8)

A student chose Matthew 28:16–20 for a consecrative sermon with the subject of evangelism. The text was presented as four commands from Jesus: "Go . . . Make disciples . . . Baptize . . . Teach." Each word was explained, but application was limited to the conclusion.

> My invitation to you is to dedicate yourselves to our Lord Jesus Christ through joining us in our mission work. We will with great joy accept your commitment as a volunteer worker for our Sunday School, or home Bible study. Join us in the tract ministry of the church.

The sermon would have been much stronger if application had been included in each part. The first point could include, "Go, as Jesus commands, to our mission point. Your participation in our tract ministry will fulfill Jesus' command to go." The preacher can tell his experience of baptizing someone he helped win to Christ through the mission point. These specific examples add interest and apply the text to the local situation.

A sermon on Isaiah 40:31 encouraged Christians to trust God during times of difficulty. The message included these phrases: "Renewed strength comes to the weary, tired, and weak. Power to rise above problems, and spiritual progress, are bestowed upon the one who trusts." The sermon lacked application to the hearers. The above statements are all true and certainly say what the text means. What does the text say to the people today in their problems? The sermon quoted parallel references to support the idea of the text. The message was weak because it remained too general and had no specific application to the people and their needs. He could have cited the difficulty of bearing with an incurable illness. What about living in a household of unbelievers?

Look to the people for life application. The prophet Ezekiel preached after he "sat among them for seven days, overwhelmed" (3:15).

Look at the Specific Objective

A clearly written specific objective encourages life application. The specific objective addresses the target audience and what you want them to do. Throughout the sermon preparation, refer to this objective. Keep it before you like a compass to give direction. Each part of the sermon should be applied to the target audience. Each point should relate to the desired result.

Matthew 3:13–17 records Jesus' baptism. A student chose the text for a sermon entitled, "Baptism: An Act of Obedience." The specific objective was "to explain the significance of baptism, and for unbaptized believers to obey Jesus and be baptized." Notice how this objective guided the application throughout his points. Observe the practical nature of this doctrinal message. It aims for decisions.

1. *Baptism follows Jesus' example* (v. 13).
   Jesus set the example; He did God's will. Will you do God's will? Follow His example and be baptized. If you are born again and still not baptized, you are disobeying Christ. You need to follow Jesus' example.

2. *Baptism fulfills all righteousness* (v. 15).
   A translation of this reads, "in this way we shall do all that God requires." Baptism is not required for salvation, but it is required for obedience to Christ. Baptism shows a right relationship has been established between you and Christ. It happened the moment you were born again. If you refuse to be baptized, something is not right between you and God. The right decision is to be baptized. Some of you have waited months, even years, since your conversion, and still have not been baptized. Is that the right thing? Is that obedience to Christ?

3. *Baptism glorifies God* (v. 17).
   If we want to glorify God, we will have to be baptized. The day you are baptized the Lord will say, as it was said to Him, "My child, My beloved! I'm pleased!" Obedience glorifies the Lord.

First Corinthians 16:1–2 served as text for a stewardship sermon, "God's Plan of Giving." The objective wanted was for "each Christian to give the tithe to the church." The sermon has four divisions and the specific objective guides the entire message. Application is achieved in several ways. Contrast the Corinthian church with your church. Tell a story about a member's experience with tithing, with his permission, of course. Give facts about some ministries that could be done when more members tithe—and when every member tithes! Show how the church meets needs that a religious television program can't.

1. *God's plan of giving involves every Christian.*
   Paul said "let each of you" give. Studies show in most churches 20 percent of the members give most of the money; 60 percent give occasionally, and 20 percent give nothing. Those statistics prevail in our church. The Lord needs each of us to support the work of our church.

2. *Giving is an act of worship.*
   When we give our gifts at church, it is like a mighty chorus of praise declaring, "Worthy is the Lamb!" You haven't worshipped completely until you give an offering.

3. *God's plan is to give through the church.*
   Since our gifts are an act of worship, they are to be presented when we gather to worship. The church is the place where the gifts are gathered. A member asked me, "Pastor, can I give my tithe to that radio preacher?" No, the tithe goes into God's storehouse, the church. Malachi 3:10 teaches this. Support your church first.

4. *God's plan of giving begins with the tithe.*
   "How much should I give?" you are asking. Paul says, "As God has prospered." The tithe—10 percent—will increase the amount as you are prospered. Jesus said of the tithe, "This you ought to have done" (Matt. 23:23). Are you tithing? Jesus said you ought! But neither should our giving stop with the tithe. We need to be careful of legalism, when giving liberally out of thanksgiving is Christ's goal. Give it as an act of worship. Do your part, and the church can do more.

Every sermon should have a specific objective which states what you want the people to do. Specific examples of this throughout the sermon will add life application.

According to Lowery, "Applied biblical preaching is effective for the congregation, but demanding for the preacher."[8] Is it wise to wait until the inspiration of the moment to think of ways to apply the text? With that approach, the sermon usually becomes overloaded with generalities. Look to the present; look to the people; look at the specific objective. An essential part of sermon preparation is life application. Haddon Robinson summed up:

> In the final analysis, effective application does not rely on techniques. It is more a stance than a method. Life-changing preaching does not talk to the people about the Bible. Instead, it talks to the people about themselves—their

questions, hurts, fears and struggles—from the Bible. When we approach the sermon with that philosophy, flint strikes steel. The flint of someone's problems strikes the steel of the Word of God, and a spark emerges that can set that person on fire for God.9

REACTION AND RESPONSE

Additional ways to increase life application in the message are found in Harold T. Bryson, and James C. Taylor, "Putting People in Sermons," *Building Sermons to Meet People's Needs*, 38–51.

Chapter 17
Illustrating the Sermon

My son bragged about a preacher at summer camp. "What made him so effective?" I asked. His response was, "He told a good story and then made a point." That shows the power of an effective illustration. The introduction, body, and conclusion of the sermon usually need an illustration. Remember, the text is always the most important element of the sermon. Three key ingredients expand the meaning of the text: explanation, illustration, and application. This chapter examines illustrations and their significant part in effective biblical preaching.

THE SIGNIFICANCE OF ILLUSTRATIONS

The best preachers are good at illustrating the sermon. The word "illustrate" means to "throw light on a subject." The illustration acts like the windows of a house and lets in light. An effective illustration helps listeners understand the message. The illustrations always support the text, thesis, objective, and divisions.

Illustrations help the listener to "see" the message. An Arab proverb says, "He is the best speaker who can turn the ear into an eye."[1] Effective communication involves several of the senses. People need to hear and see the message. Illustrations take ideas, thoughts, and teaching and put them into word pictures that people mentally see.

Communication today depends much on vision. Television influences so many. With sermon illustrations, the preacher can give a picture to express the thought. A "visual" image supports the spoken word.

Illustrations explain general concepts. Christianity is about love, faith, salvation, eternity. These teachings become more understandable with specific stories or symbols. Baptism and the Lord's Supper are acted illustrations of Christ's death for our sin. They have other purposes, also, but these two ordinances "picture" what Christ did. With them we better understand His work.

An illustration helps us remember. They are like hooks which hold the truth in our mind. When I see beautiful flowers growing in a field, I usually think of Jesus' words about worry (Matt. 7:28–31). The skill with which you connect the illustration to the point on which you want to throw light determines how well the truth will be remembered. The illustration throws light on the truth of the text, enabling us to better remember the teaching.

Illustrations touch the emotions. Emotions influence the will. We usually do what we feel like doing. The mind might be convinced, but the emotions must also be moved before people decide. With their emotions, people will also feel the message and then decide to accept it. Be cautious of extreme emotion and sentimental illustrations. People can be led to make merely an emotional decision. Jesus warned of one who "hears the word and immediately receives it with joy. Yet he has no root in himself, but endures only for a while" (Matt. 13:20–21).

An illustration acts as a pressure release. A sermon communicates truth in an intense way. Listeners may resist the message and feel pressure. A good illustration releases the pressure enough to keep attention. Humor sometimes serves this purpose in a sermon. Illustrations keep a sermon from becoming too "heavy."

These six purposes of illustrations reveal their significance for preaching. As Brown noted in *Steps to the Sermon,* "Almost all great preaching is characterized by the effective use of illustrations. The man who wishes to preach well will cultivate the art of illustrating the sermon."[2]

WHAT MAKES A GOOD ILLUSTRATION?

W. E. Sangster, 1900–1960, was a master of sermon illustrations. Born in London, England, he became president of the Methodist Conference of Great Britain. In a book about illustrations he presented seven suggestions which give helpful guidance in selecting sermon illustrations.

1. Don't confuse illustration and argument.
2. Don't make it a rule that each sermon must contain a given number of illustrations; and don't illustrate the obvious.
3. Don't labor the moral.
4. Don't forget the facts.

5. Don't glorify yourself.
6. Don't neglect the setting of your illustration.
7. Don't use illustrations that steal attention from the sermon.[3]

One preacher said, "I don't know what makes a good illustration, but I know when I've heard one." A good illustration would meet these five guidelines: supports the text, puts light on one point, is believable, understandable, and fresh.

The purpose of the illustration is to "throw light on the text." More significance rests in the text than the illustration. In a sermon on sin, I told a story which had a humorous ending; everyone laughed. The next night of the crusade, people were still talking about the story. It appeared they heard the story more than the message. It threw more light on itself than on the text. You have seen lights that burned so brightly they bothered your eyes. Instead of helping you to see, they distracted you. Reading lamps are covered to direct the light to the book being read. An illustration supports the text and does not call extra attention to itself.

A good illustration puts lights on one point. It may have several details which could be emphasized but zeroes in on the details which illustrate one point. *The Yearling*[4] tells the story of a handicapped boy and his family living near the Florida Everglades. The boy had few friends and played with the animals. An illness brought his death, and at the burial a neighbor spoke about the boy in heaven, able to walk. I used the neighbor's remarks in a sermon about heaven. The illustration would have been weakened if I had added comments about the meaning of the boy's suffering, or his father's sins. An illustration need only illuminate one point.

An illustration with several details can be used again in a sermon if it throws light on a different place. 2 Timothy 2:20–21 was the text for a sermon directed to pastors and wives. The preacher used the experience of a dinner in his home and his wife setting the table with dinner plates ("vessels for the master's use"). He noted how the plate could do nothing without the master of the house. It existed solely for the master's use. Later the dining table scene was used in another way. "What if you sat down to eat and saw the food was placed on dirty plates? You would leave thinking the Lowries were strange people. The cleanliness of the vessel reflects on the character of the owner."[5] Both uses of this common home experience are brief but effective ways to "see" the points being made.

An illustration needs to be believable. The television show *That's Incredible* looked at extraordinary people and events. I believed it when I saw it but still wondered how they did it! An illustration must be convincing. It really happened or could happen. A sermon should not create the attitude of "make-believe" or fantasy. Believable illustrations show the life applications of the text.

A Mother's Day sermon included the story of an eagle that swooped down and flew away with a baby, taking it to a lofty crag on the clift. Strong men were unable to retrieve the child, but the mother, driven by love, persevered up the dangerous heights to rescue her baby. Does that sound reasonable to you? The preacher apparently had some doubts because he began the story by saying, " I don't know if this story is true or not, but it illustrates the love of a mother." It sounded more like fiction to me.

Of course, you can use fables or fiction as illustrations but identify them as such. These kinds of materials will be recognized as creative ways of illustrating.

A successful newspaper editor lost his job when it was discovered he had written stories about his war record which were not true. They sounded believable but were false. Telling an illustration so that it appears to have happened to you, when it really didn't, doesn't add to your integrity.

Historical and scientific information make good illustration material. Check the accuracy of your facts. Scientific data used in a sermon ten to fifteen years ago may very likely have changed.

An effective illustration begins at the level of understanding. It uses something known to throw light on the unknown or unaccepted. Use facts about the universe and stars in a sermon on Psalm 8. The listeners may not know these facts nor understand astronomy, but they see the stars and the moon. The subject of your illustration is known and used to throw light on the theme of your sermon, God's creative power.

An illustration may sound good, but will it be understood? Published sermons, first preached in another context, contain some good illustrations. People in your church may not understand them because the material fits another culture. An American preached in a crusade in Brazil with his sermon translated into Portugese. To illustrate one point the preacher told a humorous story. It was funny back in Texas but not understood in Brazil. Instead of telling the story the translator said to the people in Portugese, "He told a funny story, please laugh!"

When our family lived in the Philippines, I discovered dinuguan (blood pudding) was a favorite dish of many nationals. Filipino friends reminded me if I wanted to try it to "be sure and make it with fresh ingredients." Good advice for cooking and preaching! Fresh illustrations make better sermons. General MacArthur's famous words upon leaving Bataan, "I will return," have been used in many sermons about Christ's return. The incident has lost its fresh quality. Frequent use and time have robbed it of some power and freshness. More people in the congregation now identify with Vietnam and the Persian Gulf crisis.

The introduction of a Father's Day sermon included this personal experience.

> One afternoon while I was cutting the grass in the backyard, our four-year-old daughter, Mary, came to the door and shouted, "Daddy, how do you spell love?" I gave her the four letters. I was later surprised to receive a card from her, and on it she had printed, "I Love You."

How do you spell love? It is more than putting four letters of the alphabet in correct order. We spell love as we live it and express it in our relationships. In that way, love may be the most misspelled word in the vocabulary of our life.

How do you spell love? Our children are asking. A world in need of Christ's love watches and waits for our response.

The illustration was similar to the experience of many in the congregation. It moved from the known to introduce the unknown—the sermon topic. It made only one point, supported the text (the next paragraph moved into the text), and had a fresh quality about it.

A good illustration supports the text and throws light on one point only. Effective illustrations are believable, understandable, and fresh. Do the following illustrations achieve these qualities? Remember the best evaluation comes from seeing how they are used in an actual sermon.

Thankful

The word tells us to "give thanks in all circumstances" (1 Thess. 5:18). A blind businessman I met one day was able to do what Paul said. He told me, "I don't think about what I have lost. I'm just thankful for what I still have."

Stewardship

A Cadillac went by me on the interstate bearing the license tag "ALL HIS." Did that mean his wife had a BMW at home with a tag "HERS"? Had he just paid off an installment loan taken out when the car was bought? Could the driver have been a newly retired pastor, taking a long-deserved vacation in his retirement gift? Did the deacons think the tag summed up the pastor's dedication to Christ? Did the tag represent a man's selfish attitude toward possessions, or the testimony of a Christian who had dedicated his car to Christ? Does the use of our possessions bear witness that everything we have belongs to the Lord. Would we be honest in saying it's ALL HIS?

Cross

A thirty-eight-year-old carpenter, Donald Rexford Jr., allowed himself to be nailed to a cross and hoisted into the air for 2 minutes before hundreds of onlookers in a Good Friday reenactment of the crucifixion in Manila, Philippines. He has done this for many years as an act of penance. His suffering is useless. Jesus offered Himself "once for all" (Heb. 10:10) as a free gift to be received by faith.[7]

Speech

James 3:2–12 reminds us of the difficulty in controlling the tongue. Some members of a Singapore construction firm devised a method to help improve their language. Whenever bad language occurs, workers pay about $1.00 into a "swear box." A construction manager confessed, "We have become so used to using swear words that they come out often when we speak. They can be embarrassing." During the first four days the "swear box" collected about $23.00.[5]

Love

A gift shop featured a Valentine window display with a large black heart trimmed in lace. The designer failed in his attempt to show love. The black heart seemed to represent a lack of love. An absence of real love leaves life dark, lonely, and lifeless. Christ cited love as a characteristic of his disciples (John 13:34). When we share His love, it is like a transfusion of life into hearts black with sin, loneliness, and defeat.

FINDING SERMON ILLUSTRATIONS

Sermon illustrations come from the same sources as sermon ideas mentioned in chapter 7. Ten major sources offer endless variety for preaching.

The Bible

A preacher wrote an older minister asking him to recommend a book of illustrations. "The Bible" was the reply. The Bible offers an unending source for sermon illustrations. Bible illustrations add authority to the message, and they will be familiar to most people. Bible personalities mirror every kind of action and attitude, illustrating the good and the bad results of life decisions you will preach about.

Nave's Topical Bible lists topics or subjects alphabetically and becomes a resource for locating Bible illustrations. Of course, the context of the references will need to be examined to see if it fits your sermon.

Observation

Observation is our most valuable source for illustrations. An excellent preacher described this as "the harvest of the eye."[8] Jesus made his disciples aware of their weakness in observing spiritual lessons in the events of life. On two occasions they saw Him feed the mulitudes with a few loaves and fish. These were lessons to trust Him and to seek eternal values. They didn't see it. He said to them:

> Why do you reason because you have no bread? Do you not yet perceive nor understand? Is your heart still hardened? Having eyes do you not yet see? (Mark 8:17–18)

You may never be able to have a large library, but you can "read" the events happening around you. What do they say about the text? Use your eyes and ears and observe life for the best illustrations.

On my way to church one day in Manila, I noticed some men in their swimming trunks, bathing at a corner fire hydrant, which is a fairly common sight in Philippine cities where many homes are without water. I walked past them and then saw, on the opposite corner, the sewer overflowing. The contrast between filth and cleanliness reminded me of the conflict between good and evil. I told the experience in a sermon, followed by these statements.

> Which corner would you choose? Would you want to stand in the sewer? Daily our life faces the decisions of where we will stand—either for good or evil. We have to reject sin and stand for "whatever is true, right, pure, lovely, admirable." (Phil. 4:8)

Personal Experience

Your own personal experiences add sincerity and realism to the message. There is no need to apologize for using your life experiences as illustrative material. Be careful to keep the account free of pride or a superior spiritual attitude. However, your family may not like you using them as regular examples. They deserve some privacy like others in your congregation.

Never use the personal experiences of someone in your church without permission. Calling names, making an accusation, or passing judgment on others has no place in the pulpit. Using some members too often as illustrations may encourage jealousy by other members.

Biography and Autobiography

Biography and autobiography supply interesting sermon material. A biography of Winston Churchill describes the days prior to World War II when England's leaders followed a policy of appeasing Hitler, hoping to avert war. Churchill was one of a few who called for his countrymen to stand against the German tyrant. With Hitler's armies poised to seize Czechoslovakia, Churchill tried to secure the signatures of several leaders on a telegram imploring Prime Minister Chamberlain to make no more concessions. The group drifted away, and no telegram was sent. Churchill said: "What are they made of? The day is not far off when it won't be signatures we'll have to give but lives—the lives of millions. Can we survive? Do we deserve to do so when there's no courage anywhere?"[9]

The lives of faithful Christians illuminate a text. The story of missionary William Carey will illustrate many mission sermons. An event from the life of English preacher Charles Spurgeon is used in support of Romans 16:1–16 in a sermon entitled "Ordinary Christians."

> Who led you to Christ? For most of us, they were ordinary people of our lives—our parents, ministers, Sunday School teachers, deacons, friends. Most of the work of Christ is carried on by the ordinary Christians living out their lives in routine ways. Charles Spurgeon, who became one of the most noted preachers of the last century, was converted under the preaching of a lay preacher. Spurgeon turned into a little Primitive Methodist Church on a side street in London when a heavy snowstorm hit. Only about a dozen or fifteen people were present. Even the regular preacher could not make it. A thin-looking man, a tailor or shoemaker, was preaching. His text was "Look unto me, and be ye saved, all ye ends of the earth" (Isa. 45:22). Spurgeon said the man could not even pronounce the words correctly, but he noted that the text called upon persons to look unto Jesus. Finally, the preacher turned to Spurgeon and fixed his eyes upon him and declared, "Young man, you look miserable. And you will always look miserable—miserable in life, miserable in death—if you don't obey my text; but if you obey now, this moment, you will be saved." The preacher then lifted his hand and shouted: "Young man, look to Jesus Christ. Look! Look! Look! You have nothing to do but to look and live." Spurgeon said that he saw at once the way of salvation, and the cloud of darkness rolled away from his life, and he saw the sun. An ordinary Christian layman had led this young man to Christ.
>
> Romans 16 is filled with the names of early Christian leaders who were the ordinary people God used in the first century to share his good news. Most of them are only names to us, but they were God's servants, like we are today, spreading the good news of Christ with others.[10]

Literature

The many kinds of literature give variety to sermon illustrations. Fiction books describe life, often in vivid language.

Poetry expresses ideas and throws light on sermon points. These lines were kept for a sermon I later preached when I moved to a new location.

> To me remains nor place nor time;
> My country is in every clime;
> I can be calm and free from every care
> On any shore, since God is there.

While place we seek, or place we shun,
The soul finds happiness in none;
But with a God to guide our way,
'Tis equal joy to go or stay.[11]

Newspapers and Magazines

Newspaper and magazines contain many illustrations from daily life. The editorial page and cartoons also offer illustrations. The Sunday magazine frequently has personal interest stories that may be used to illustrate your sermon topics. A quick glance through the Sunday paper before you leave for a preaching assignment sometimes brings a very contemporary illustration for that day's sermon.

Urban pastor Bill Hybels believes most unchurched people think Christians, especially pastors, "are woefully out of touch with reality. That's why I select 60 to 70 percent of my illustrations from current events. I read *Time, Newsweek, U.S. News & World Report, Forbes,* and usually, *Business Week*." Every day he reads a local paper and watches at least two television news programs. Why? "Because when I can use a contemporary illustration, I build credibility. The unchurched person says, 'He's in the same world I'm in.'"[12]

Radio and Television

Radio and television programs describe daily life and current events. Commentators quote a leader, tell about an event, describe current trends, or make life observations that add spice to sermons. Televison shows that dramatize history or depict a social problem may be a window to offer light for your preaching. For several days the country's attention riveted on the rescue of a little Texas girl who fell into a well shaft in her backyard. Television, newspapers, and magazines, told the story. It included many examples on the value of life, courage, determination. One sermon pointed out the contrast between the way some supported abortion but wanted every effort made to save a young child.

Scientific Facts

Scientific information also supplies effective sermon illustrations. A message on Romans 13:11–14 shows how a preacher saw spiritual truth in scientific facts about an insect.

> The cattle tick is a little bloodsucking insect with an amazing life history. When it comes from the egg, the tick is not fully developed. It does not have legs, nor can it reproduce. Even in that state it can attack cold-blooded

animals. . . . The female has no eyes. She is directed to the tip of a twig on a bush by her skin which is photosensitive. She stays on the edge of that bush through night and day, cold weather and hot, waiting for the moment she can fulfill her purpose in life.

In a zoo these female cattle ticks have been observed to stay on the end of twigs for eighteen years! Eighteen years of waiting for just the right moment! Eighteen years of doing nothing but waiting. That tick waits for the scent of sweat in all animals. And when a person or a dog walks by that twig, for the first time in her life that tick's reason for living has come! She leaps on to that animal, buries herself in the flesh, and does what she is supposed to do.

[The pastor preaching this sermon had been pastor at his church for 18 years.] When are you going to get off your twig and do what you were meant to do?! Paul echoed this need for urgency when he told the Romans it was time to wake from sleep, throw off the works of darkness, and be busy about the work Christ had for them.[13]

When you use illustrations from science, be sure you have correct facts.

Music

Lines from popular music get attention from the listeners and support a point. I overheard a song my teenage daughter was listening too. The lines became the introduction to a sermon and were used again in the conclusion. "There's got to be a way to connect this world today. There's got to be a way to unite this human race and together we'll bring on a change."[14] I noticed the heightened interest of teenagers in the audience. Remember, Paul quoted a pagan poet when he spoke to the Athenians. Christian hymns have long been used as sermon illustrations. The story of how a hymn was written may prove effective.

Sermon Books

I find sermon books another source for illustrations. After I study the text and get an outline, I sometimes look in other sermons for appropriate illustrations. Be certain the illustration throws light on your text; it might be appropriate in the printed sermon but not really support yours.

These ten sources of illustrations will supply you with material that will make your sermons more interesting and applicable to life. As you read and study, make notes of illustrations you can use later. Reference them by subject and/or Scripture text. Maintain the file for easy access when you are preparing to preach.

DIMMING THE LIGHT

We need to consider three inappropriate uses of sermon illustrations which frequently occur in preaching. Awareness of these helps maintain the intensity of the light thrown by an illustration. Illustrations lose their power when they violate the guidelines presented in the first part of this chapter. Effectiveness further declines with these typical abuses: (1) talking about the illustration, (2) a lack of variety, and (3) the number of illustrations used.

Work to avoid the common practice of talking about the illustration. The force of the illustration decreases when you make unimportant, unnecessary comments about it. Some examples of these comments are:

- You may have heard this story before . . .
- I can't remember if I've told you this . . .
- Excuse me for telling a personal experience . . .
- I'm not very good at telling stories . . .
- Bro. White told me this recently, but I don't think he'll mind my telling you.
- Let me illustrate this point.
- This may illustrate what I'm trying to say.

When a light needs to be turned on in a room, do you explain where you bought the lamp, how long you have used it, or what voltage it is? An illustration, like a light, speaks for itself and needs no explanation or apologetic comments. You do not need to say, "I got this illustration from a book I read this week." Use the illustration in a natural, supportive way. Instead of talking about the illustration, say only what is necessary for understanding.

Sometimes you may need to cite the source of the illustration, especially if you need to add authority and make the illustration stronger. The source of a quote was given in this sermon introduction.

> Richard Foster, in a significant book entitled *Celebration of Discipline*, has written: "In contemporary society our Adversary majors in three things: noise, hurry, and crowds. If he can keep us engaged in 'muchness' and 'manyness,' he will rest satisfied." One of the greatest needs of believers in our world is to plan times of solitude.[15]

It would have been dishonest for the preacher to use the words from the book as if they were his own. He did not make any unnecessary comments such as, "I've been reading this book," or "Richard Foster is a Quaker, but we Baptists can learn something from him." Unnecessary comments about your illustrations decrease the light they throw and detract the people's attention. Don't talk about your illustration, just illustrate.

A second misuse of illustrations is a lack of variety. A message with all the illustrations from the same type of source lowers the interest. A student preached a good sermon on the subject, "Triumph in Trials." In the sermon, three illustrations were used of people who overcame their trials. These examples were a famous American black educator, the blind songwriter Fanny Crosby, and a medical doctor. All three were good illustrations, but each was wealthy or widely known. A congregation of lower educated or poor people would not have identified with the examples, or possibly marked them off by saying, "They've got plenty of money to overcome. We don't."

If you use personal experiences in every sermon the people may think you are "preaching yourself." I knew a pastor who illustrated most of his sermons with events, people, and circumstances from his previous place of service. The people began to feel his heart was back there instead of with them. He needed variety in his illustrations. One member described her pastor, "He would have made a good sportscaster, he's always telling about sports." Members who cared little about sports or did not understand the plays and rules were turned off by his lack of variety.

Calvin Miller, especially gifted in illustrative material, showed variety in an Easter sermon.[16]

- a John Updike quotation
- a phrase from P. T. Barnum
- the response of his sister when he announced his call to preach
- a news story about UFOs
- an experience he and his wife had
- an incident from the life of Charles Colson
- a story from radio commentator Paul Harvey
- the contrast between a taxidermined lifeguard and a living lifeguard
- an Eva McAllaster poem
- strong verbs and visually interesting language

Sermon illustrations should relate to the variety of people who hear the message. A church located in a coal mining area doesn't need to hear all illustrations based on the life of the western plains, nor most of them from the coal mining industry. Communities have variety; look for it and capitalize on it in preaching. Jesus' illustrations are of varied interests, appealing to a homemaker, a farmer, a businessman, a fisherman, and a shepherd.

- light on a stand — Matthew 5:15
- sowing seed — Matthew 13:3
- landowner and his workers — Matthew 25:14
- fishing — Luke 5:10
- lost sheep — Luke 15:3
- cleaning house — Luke 15:8

All of these illustrations come from daily life. The "harvest of the eye" gleaned spiritual lessons in the common experiences of people. Do not secure all your illustrations from the same source. Variety will make the sermon more interesting and appeal to more people.

A third misuse of illustrations is the number used. How many illustrations are needed in a sermon? No rule applies to every message. A sermon can have too many or not enough. Plan and use the best illustrations you have. Remember the purpose of an illustration is to "throw light on a subject." If the point is clear enough, don't use an illustration.

The sermon proclaims God's word. Too many illustrations crowd out the Bible teaching. Some sermons use so many illustrations that the message becomes a group of pleasant stories loosely connected by a thread of Bible truth. Beware of becoming a "storyteller" rather than a preacher of the Word.

Not enough illustrations also weaken the sermon. A student preached on Psalm 51. He faithfully interpreted the text and had excellent content. The problem of sin, need for confession, and the assurance of forgiveness were depicted in David's life. The sermon needed other illustrations of how these truths worked. David was one example but was not contemporary. Other sins can illustrate the tragic consequences of disobeying God. Those who had never committed adultery might tune out, thinking "This sermon isn't for me." The testimony of a convert could show the joy of confession and restoration. Use enough illustrations to throw light on the subject, show its application to life today, and keep people interested. Those who heard the sermon on Psalm 51 felt it was "long." It really wasn't, but the lack of illustrations made it seem longer.

Illustrations help us personally apply the truth of God's Word to our congregations. "Five-star generalizers in the pulpit resemble hovercrafts that skim across the bay but never touch down anywhere."[17] All around us are places to touch down with relevant, contemporary illustrations anywhere we preach. On a preaching mission to northern Nigeria, I traveled a bumpy dirt road to a remote village. I had been told the people of the village had a great concern for power, and my sermon that night had that theme, especially the power to overcome sin and have the new life in Christ. I wanted illustrations

Illustrating the Sermon

of power they would understand. We crossed a riverbed whose banks gave evidence of the power of the spring rains and floods. The hot wind from the desert and their custom of burning the fields in preparation for harvest provided other places to touch down with relevance. Look for the illustrations in your setting and the people will "hear you gladly."

REACTION AND RESPONSE

Evaluate the illustrations used in the last three messages you preached. Were they believable, understandable, and fresh? Did you use a variety of sources with which the congregation could identify?

Chapter 18
Just Imagine

By the gate, hugging his mantle close, the watchman walked. At times he stopped, attracted by a stir among the sleeping herds, or by a jackal's cry off on the mountainside. The midnight was slow coming to him, but at last it came. His task was done; now for the dreamless sleep with which labor blesses its wearied children! He moved towards the fire but paused; a light was breaking around him, soft and white, like the moon's. He waited breathlessly. The light deepened; things before invisible came to view; he saw the whole field, and all it sheltered. A chill sharper than that of the frosty air—a chill of fear—smote him. He looked up; the stars were gone; the light was dropping as from a window in the sky; as he looked it became a splendor; then, in terror, he cried:

"Awake, awake!"

Up sprang the dogs, and, howling, ran away. The herds rushed together, bewildered. The men clambered to their feet, weapons in hand.

"What is it?" they asked, in one voice.

"See!" cried the watchman, "the sky is on fire!"

Suddenly the light became intolerably bright, and they covered their eyes and dropped upon their knees; then, as their souls shrank with fear, they fell upon their faces blind and fainting, and would have died had not a voice said to them:

Just Imagine

"Fear not!"

And they listened.

"Fear not; for behold, I bring you good tidings of great joy, which shall be to all people."

With imaginative language Lew Wallace[1] pictured the possible scene when the angels declared Christ's birth to the shepherds. His use of imagination helped the book *Ben Hur* become a classic.

Sermon illustrations and imagination are closely related. With imagination the text can be explained and illustrated. With imagination you use your mind to think of ways to describe events, people, and emotions. Imagination "pictures" your ideas. Developing your imagination will add light to your messages. A dictionary defines imagination as "the picturing power or act of the mind; the constructive or creative faculty . . . imagination is deep, essential, spiritual . . . imagination goes to the heart of things, and is deep, earnest, serious, and seeks always and everywhere for essential truth."[2]

Imagination is "thinking by seeing."[3] With imagination, facts and ideas are clothed with pictures. Imagination brings from the storehouse of your mind experiences and pictures to illustrate an idea, a teaching, or a subject. The mental material is real and understandable. Imagination takes this mental material and paints new pictures.

Apply your imagination to the historical events presented in a text. Acts 8:26–40 includes several facts about the Ethiopian and the circumstances of his life and the period in which he lived. Imagination can express these facts in pictures that can make the passage "come alive" for the listener.

> Imagine the "desert road." The heat of the sun ran a steady stream of sweat down his back. But he never noticed. His heart was being warmed more by the words of the prophet. His forehead wrinkled with misunderstanding; how he wished for someone to help him understand this book.

> This Ethiopian knew plenty about finances but little about God. But God knew him. As surely as his chariot rolled through the soft sand, God was patiently working to lead this government official into the light of truth.

The passage overflows with other details that can feed your imagination. "One can only make history real by imaginative revival in his own mind of the scenes, persons, and events of the past, by thinking oneself back into a period, or bringing it forward to our own time."[4]

Apply imagination to the emotions of the people described in the text. Imagine how they felt. Feel their motivation. Was Philip hesitant to witness to such an important official? Did he wonder what he might say? Was he fearful of saying the wrong thing? The text says the Ethiopian "went on his way rejoicing" (v. 39). Imagine the difference in the remainder of his trip! Did he witness to the chariot driver and other helpers in the group? No doubt he thought of many in Ethiopia who would be glad to hear this "good news." With imagination the preacher tries to put himself in the place of others. Try to imagine how the biblical person might think or act. That is different from the way you would think or act if you were there.

One person with a fine imagination was described: "She had the secret not only of reading the hearts of men, but of creeping into their skins, watching the world with their eyes."[5]

Broadus suggested five ways to develop the imagination.[6] Study nature and art to get more facts about the world. The world around us contains spiritual truths: "The heavens declare the glory of God" (Ps. 19:1). Look for the spiritual lessons in nature.

Study literature that depends on imagination. The creative minds of writers, artists, and musicians help us see the values hidden in life. These writers use picture language, and we can learn by their example. Reading gives us ideas, creative words, and expressions. Develop your imagination through a variety of reading. The literature that moves the emotions will be most helpful.

Keep close to the people, especially your church members. Visitation and fellowship with those to whom you preach will stir your mind to thinking about their concerns.

Keep spiritually close to the Lord. Waiting upon the Lord, faithfulness in prayer, meditation on the word, and growing faith are ingredients to move the imagination.

Most of us don't use our imagination. As Broadus put it, "We must begin where we are and do always the best we can." Your imagination may not be as good as someone else's, but begin to use it. Everyone has some ability to use his imagination, and the Lord has promised to increase our abilities when we use them faithfully.

A student showed imagination in an illustration describing the meeting of two friends. "The sight of his old friend made him so happy, his heart seemed to applaud with excitement." Words are the preacher's servants. Use them to picture your ideas. Stott wrote, "It is by imagination that men have lived; imagination rules our lives. The human mind is not . . . a debating hall, but a picture gallery."[7]

Some will probably protest the use of imagination. "You're adding to the Word of God." If you honestly describe the biblical event with such prefaces as, "I can picture this in my mind," or "I imagine," you have been faithful to the text. Surely folks are aware we don't have "The Rest of the Story" told in the brief account contained in Scripture.

REACTION AND RESPONSE

Study the use of imagination in Fred Craddock's message, "Have You Ever Heard John Preach?" in James W. Cox, ed., *Best Sermons 4* (Harper: San Francisco, 1991), 10–17.

Unit 6

Sermon Workshop

In chapter 11 you learned six major objectives for preaching. You will preach all these varieties of sermons because each type meets a life need of the people with whom you work. This textbook is limited to a closer look at only four of these major objectives.

Evangelism seeks to bring people to a saving knowledge of the Lord Jesus Christ and into the fellowship of the church. "Preaching the gospel" often carries the connotation of preaching an evangelistic message. Whenever we preach the Bible, we are proclaiming good news. Doctrine, ethics, or pastoral care derive their meaning from the saving work of Christ. Only one with assurance of salvation and living under the Lordship of Christ can fully appropriate these other dimensions of biblical truth. My daughter and I were talking about preaching and she expressed the feeling, "The preacher should say something for the benefit of those who are not Christians." Yet a preacher who offers evangelistic messages as the sole item on his homiletical menu will find his people malnourished and in danger of spiritual defeat. Realism demands we face the fact that few lost people attend our regular worship, and most who come to profess Christ have had previous personal work. The pastor-preacher's evangelism work must go far beyond preaching.

Evangelism in its broadest terms includes discipleship. Thus the need for messages on biblical doctrines and ethics. We've often heard the church stands one generation from extinction; just let this one quit telling the story. How will they tell if they do not know? Who will believe us if the ethics of Christ does not rule our lives? Teaching and preaching are closely linked in building the body of Christ and fulfilling His mission.

How can the body do its work when there is illness? We are called to "bear one another's burdens." The preacher-pastor shepherds the flock and, from the Word of God, imparts comfort and hope. Preaching has the best hearing when it comes from a shepherd-pastor whom the people know loves them and lives out that love through personal involvement in the lives of his people.

Chapter 19
Evangelistic Preaching

The evangelistic sermon has as its main objective bringing the unsaved to Jesus Christ and the unchurched into a fellowship of faith. Through evangelistic preaching we fulfill Jesus' command, "Follow me, and I will make you become fishers of men" (Mark 1:17). Unsaved people who hear you preach will need to know how to be born again. Evangelism includes presenting the good news of Jesus, asking people to trust Him as the only way of salvation and to follow Him obediently in baptism, uniting with a New Testament church for nurture and growth.

The target audience for evangelistic sermons includes the unsaved and those who have not been baptized and become part of a church. Aim the message toward those individuals. The specific objective for each evangelistic sermon should be aimed toward the unsaved and unbaptized.

In the first chapter of this textbook you learned about the Greek word *euaggelizo*. It means "to tell the good news or good tidings" and refers to the message preached. Evangelistic preaching emphasizes the good news of Jesus' death and resurrection for people's sin. Evangelistic sermons present Jesus' work to redeem (save) all people. An evangelistic message shows people what they have done wrong, but also presents the "good news" of Jesus Christ, "the way, the truth and the life." A good doctor determines why one is sick but also prescribes a cure. A sermon that only condemns sin and the sinner but offers no hope is unbalanced and fails as evangelistic preaching. Jesus said, "God did not send his Son into the world to condemn the world, but that the world through Him might be saved" (John 3:17). Evangelism presents the whole story of what Jesus did to solve the sin problem.

Evangelistic preaching includes an appeal to repent—turn away—from sin and trust Christ. All biblical preaching should "urgently appeal for the hearers to respond positively to the will of God." (Recall that definition from unit 1?) The specific response desired from evangelistic preaching is repentance toward God and faith in Jesus as the only Savior (Acts 20:21).

God decided through "the foolishness of what was preached to save those who believe" (1 Cor. 1:21). Evangelistic preaching holds an essential part in God's plan of salvation. When the gospel, the power of God unto salvation (Rom. 1:16–17), is preached, a person hears in faith, and the power of the gospel accomplishes salvation in the person's heart. Stephen Olford noted, "With the proclamation there is the declaration of that which God has done and is doing in Christ and His cross; then the invitation calls men and women to respond to this Good News. If this is not our motive, then our preaching will be powerless and fruitless. God never releases His power for personal aggrandizement or carnal objectives; on the contrary, He only sends His Holy Spirit to seal unto the day of redemption that which fulfills His redemptive purposes."[1]

A student prepared the following evangelistic sermon outline with balanced content. Sin and the Savior are included. The hearers are asked to repent and trust Christ. The third point needs to include some description of the results which followed the Ethiopian's faith response. This message is good news!

THE SEARCHING GOD (ACTS 8:26–39)

I. The searching God seeks lost sinners (vv. 26–29).
God takes the first step to bring you back into fellowship with Him. He sought the religious Ethiopian. He was a good man, a religious man, but he was a sinner without Christ.

II. God searches with several means to find you (vv. 26–39).
  1. He uses the guidance of the Spirit (vv. 26, 29).
  2. He uses the Word (vv. 32, 39).
  3. He uses His messengers (vv. 26, 35).

III. The searching God demands your deliberate response (vv. 36–39).
Either reject Him or accept Him. The Ethiopian believed Christ. Admit you are a lost sinner and trust Christ who died in your place.

Acts 16:25–34 offers a good text for an evangelistic sermon. The message includes the problem of sin, the way to solve the problem, and the evidence of genuine response. This outline keeps the focus on the jailer, moving from his life before and after Christ. The text includes details that offer fertile ground for the imagination.

Evangelistic Preaching 145

A JAILER SET FREE (ACTS 16:25–34)

I. The jailer is a prisoner of life and death (vv. 25–27).
The jailer was a man afraid to live and not ready to die. His fear of facing his superiors made him want to kill himself. Without Christ, he was not ready to die. He held the keys to the jail but was imprisoned by his own fear and uncertainty.

II. The jailer realized his need of freedom (vv. 28–29).
He realized Paul and Silas had something he didn't have. Why had they not fled? He recalled their attitude when placed in the cell; he remembered their singing.

III. The jailer heard the message of freedom (vv. 31–32).
He was told to "believe in the Lord Jesus Christ." The apostles "spoke the word of the Lord" unto him. Paul and Silas told him about Jesus' death and resurrection. They encouraged him to repent and believe the gospel.

IV. The jailer found freedom (vv. 33–34).
He and others in his family "had come to believe in God." His life was changed. He showed his obedience by baptism and a new attitude toward his prisoners. Joy filled the house!

The message included a "now" quality by using other testimonies of changed lives. Of course, everything the jailer did needed also to be done by individuals present in the church who did not know Christ. Sermons on Bible personalities sometimes remain in the past. The above sermon could be made more contemporary by rephrasing the divisions to fit anyone in need of Christ. Use contemporary examples of the scriptural pattern and principles. A contemporary retelling of Matthew 25:14–30 went like this:

> A rich CEO goes off on a business trip. Before leaving for Dulles, he gives each of three employees a fair amount of money to invest. On his return, he asks for an accounting. The first two have done fabulously at the stock exchange; their investment has doubled. "Well done, gentlemen!" Up comes employee number three. "Sir, all of us know you're a hard man to please. I was afraid, so I hid your money; here it is, exactly what you gave me." The CEO blows a final fuse, "You worthless piece of garbage! Out you go into the darkness!"[2]

One student chose Luke 16:19–31 for an evangelistic sermon entitled "Life after Death." His written objective targeted the message toward "people" rather than unsaved people. Not until the last paragraph of the sermon did he state what he desired, "Come to Jesus just as you are and you will be saved."

"Turning from Tradition to Truth," based on Acts 2:36–47, had a specific objective "that lost sinners repent from their sins and accept Christ as Lord and become a member of a local church." The student's outline reflected this objective. This message was preached in an area with many people of strong religious tradition but lacking a personal relationship with Christ. Thus the emphasis on tradition. Notice how the third division includes the discipleship aspect of evangelism.

TURNING FROM TRADITION TO TRUTH (ACTS 2: 36–47)

   I. Turn to the truth about sin (vv. 36, 39–40).
   Traditonal religious leaders cried out, "Crucify him!" Sin crucified Christ. Tradition may explain away our wrong, but the truth is we are all sinners, part of a "corrupt generation."
   II. Turn to Jesus, who is the Truth (vv. 38–39).
   Christ did what tradition could not do. Accept his salvation by repenting. Be baptized into Christ and not into religious tradition.
   III. Turn to the church that is upholding the truth (42–47).
   The church is for those who are saved. Christ's plan for those who accept Him is for the new believer to become a member of a local church. Believers identify with a fellowship of Christian followers.

The objective of an evangelistic sermon is to bring the unsaved to Jesus Christ and into the fellowship of the local church. Such a sermon contains both the truth about sin and the solution Jesus offers. It should always contain an appeal for repentance and faith.

The following sermon offers a case study in the principles of this textbook. "Rescue the Perishing" was preached in a county seat, college town First Baptist Church during a Sunday morning service. It shows how doctrine can be preached with an evangelistic purpose. Remember that a printed message never reflects the personality of the preacher, the tone of the voice, nor the uniqueness of the moment.

RESCUE THE PERISHING (JOHN 3:16 RSV)[3]

An old tale describes a man who habitually read the obituaries the first thing each morning. If his name was not listed, he dressed and went to work. One morning he read the obituaries and discovered his name among them. Of course, he was shaken but decided to go to work anyway. Once at work he

Evangelistic Preaching

called a friend and asked: "Did you read my name in the obituaries this morning?" "Yes," said his friend, "Where are you calling from?"

Where? John 3:16 notes two possibilities in the words perish and eternal life. The Bible teaches that beyond death we live in a state of conscious existence either with God or without God. In this message we will consider the destiny of the perishing.

Present Condition
The Scripture tells us that this word described a present condition. Paul wrote, "The word of the cross is folly to those who are perishing" (1 Cor. 1:18). He equates unbelievers and the perishing: "If our gospel is veiled, it is veiled only to those who are perishing . . . the god of this world has blinded the minds of the unbelievers, to keep them from seeing the light of the gospel of the glory of Christ" (2 Cor. 4:3).

Anyone who has refused Jesus as Lord and Savior is presently perishing. Luke 15 records three parables of the lost sheep, the lost coin, and the lost boy. The English word "lost" is the same Greek word found in John 3:16, "perish." Broken fellowship, lost usefulness, and open rebellion all depict the perishing condition of an individual without Christ.

A young man at the University of Pennsylvania printed the words "Life Is Hell" on a card and put it on his desk. Every time he studied he saw those words. One morning they found his body. He'd gotten up from his desk and jumped out the window. Many live each day in a hellish, perishing kind of existence. It doesn't have to be that way. We do not have to perish but can have an abundant life. Jesus said, "I came that they may have life, and have it abundantly" (John 10:10). We were made to live, not die. Belief in Jesus, who died for our sin, takes one from among the dead into the land of the living.

Eternal Consequence
Perishing is a present condition but also an eternal consequence. Hebrews 9:27 says, "It is appointed for men to die once, and after that comes judgment." The judgment of the unbeliever is to eternally perish. Jesus used a vivid and terrible picture to warn people of this eternal consequence. Outside the city walls of Jerusalem was the Valley of Hinnon. During the reign of Ahaz and Manasseh, children were offered there as burnt sacrifices to appease heathen idols. Under Josiah these altars were destroyed and the valley declared unclean. It later became a dumping place for rubbish, city garbage, and dead beggars.

Fires burned continually. Jesus chose the worst visual aid people could see to warn of the eternal consequence waiting those who reject Him.

A feature story in the newspaper asked the question, "Whatever Happened to Hell?"[4] The reporter noted increasing skepticism and doubt of this biblical teaching. Raymond Moody in *Life After Life* reports on out-of-body experiences of people who were "dead" and revived on the operating table. These reports have created a vision of eternity as only bright lights and beautiful music. I'll take my knowledge of what is beyond death from the One who said, "I am the first and the last, and the living one; I died, and behold I am alive for evermore, and I have the keys of Death" (Rev. 1:17–18).

Do you believe in hell, the eternal consequence for the unbeliever? It seems we hold to this more in theory than in practice. Would we have so many unsaved youth if Christian parents really believed in hell? The reality of an old hymn needs to grip us and motivate us to rescue the perishing.

> Brethren, see poor sinners round you
> Slumb'ring on the brink of woe;
> Death is coming, hell is moving,
> Can you bear to let them go?
> See our fathers and our mothers,
> And our children sinking down.[5]

To know about hell and be silent is a gross sin of omission. Warn! Plead! Rescue the perishing; snatch them in pity from sin and the grave!

Individual Choice

A third truth about this word perish is noted many times in God's Word. This condition and consequence is forced upon no one; it is a matter of choice. Jesus said, "It is not the will of my Father who is in heaven that one . . . should perish" (Matt. 18:14). He also said, "Eternal fire (is) prepared for the devil and his angels" (Matt. 25:41). Heaven is prepared for the redeemed; the choice is ours. "Whoever believes" is the only condition; Jesus is the only way. "How shall we escape if we neglect such a great salvation?" (Heb. 2:3).

Jesus once told of two men who had little in common (Luke 16:19–31). One was clothed in fine linen, the other in rags. The rich man had everything he wanted; the beggar didn't even have what he needed. One dined on delicate cuisine; the other went hungry with dirty crumbs. The doctors treated the rich man, while the dogs licked the beggar's sores. So far apart, but at one point both men occupied the same position: "the poor man died . . . the rich man also died." Death clears our calendars, stops the process of decision, and equalizes men. Jesus gave each man's eternal destiny: "the rich man . . . in Hades . . . Lazarus in (Abraham's) bosom."

What determined their destiny? A decision made "in your lifetime." The rich man lived for self and time, ignoring God and eternity. He pled for Lazarus to be sent to his five remaining brothers, warning them to avoid hell. It could not be done. "They have Moses and the prophets; let them hear them." "Faith comes by hearing and hearing by the word of God" (Rom. 10:17). God's Word has told you of an eternal destiny; now you must decide. God has made a way, but if you choose your way He will abide by your decision. He gives the freedom of choice. C. S. Lewis said, "In the end there will be two kinds of persons—those who say to God: 'Thy will be done,' and those to whom God says: 'Thy will be done.'" Deciding for Christ can change your present condition into an abundant life and seal your eternal destiny with God. What a tremendous promise: "God so loved the world, that He gave His only begotten Son, that whosoever believeth in Him should not perish, but have eternal life."

This message, one of a series based on John 3:16, focuses on the word perish and the awful reality of rejecting Christ. With a one-verse text, does this message qualify as an expository sermon? Robinson notes such a sermon "can be expository if it derives its content and development from the wider context or thought. A sermon cannot be called expository which merely tips the hat to the context or ignores it completely and uses the single verse as a launching pad for the preacher's own thought."[6] The message summons the wider context and thought of New Testament teaching by references to the teaching of Jesus and Paul. Eleven other scriptural references from seven New Testament books provide support from the wider context.

The surrounding context, Nicodemus's encounter with Jesus, offers more support than the message used. Imagination could have described Nicodemus's present condition—religious but perishing. That can find plenty of application with people in the congregation. Did Nicodemus's nighttime dialogue indicate an unfulfilled search for life at its best? Do Jesus' comments about condemnation relate to the Pharisaical legalism which leaves a person feeling condemned? Many still perish while trying to live up to religious standards without any internal power to do so.

The immediate context also offers support for the third division. The individual must "be born again" (v.11). In verses 15–18, "believes in him" occurs three times.

Did the preacher of this sermon study the meaning of words and check parallel references? Note this sentence in the second division, in reference to Luke 15: "The English word 'lost' is the same Greek word found in John 3:16, 'perish.'" This was determined with an interlinear translation and a concordance. Be careful in the way you use word study in the pulpit, especially quoting original words or verb tense. Robinson tells of doing "a lot of that when I first got out of seminary."

> One day a woman wounded me with a compliment: "I just love to hear you preach. In fact, when I see the insights you get from the original languages, I realize that my English Bible is hardly worth reading."
>
> I went home asking myself, What have I done? I'm trying to get people into their Bible, but I've taken this lady out of hers.[7]

Is there a strong marriage between the idea and the text? With this message the text came first, and the preacher developed the theme, "the destiny of the perishing," from the thought of the text. The text and context support all the divisions. Unity is encouraged by using a key word throughout the sermon and alliteration on the second word of each division. The alliteration is natural for the text. Guard against an overuse of alliteration. Some members talk about trying to guess the outline or are amused with the sometimes forced usage of a word. The text should mold the outline.

Basic transition sentences connect the three divisions. The first and second divisions are connected by stating both points. The third division begins by suggesting the first two points and stating the third. The conclusion contains this summary sentence: "Deciding for Christ can change your present condition into an abundant life and seal your eternal destiny with God." The text can be restated with appropriate voice emphases on key words to stress the individual choice and the blessed results.

The title uses a well-known hymn and describes the direction and content of the message. It will look at those who perish and how they can be rescued. Another title option comes from the news story mentioned in division two, "Whatever Happened to Hell?" This has more interest and freshness and also identifies with many of the listeners' questions about eternal destiny. Either title is clear, accurate, limited, brief, and suitable.

What is your reaction to an introduction using humor? A "heavy" subject such as hell immediately faces resistance from many in the congregation. Humor touches the emotions and through that open door the preacher can enter with the truth. Another approach could show society's concern that people not perish—lifeguards at the pool, occupational safety, ICU and neonatal units at the hospital. From where does this concern come?

The message needs a more interesting thesis sentence. "Whatever happened to hell?" is one possibility. The divisions could be stated as responding to that question in these ways:

A. Some are living it right now.
B. Others will enter it at death.
C. We will make the choice.

The illustrations within this message come from a variety of sources—humor, history, newspaper, music, Scripture, and quotation from C. S. Lewis. More contemporary people-centered illustrations would help the people identify with the need and strengthen the application. Recall individuals who illustrate the perishing condition. Describe the recent choice a member made for Christ, with his permission.

Application should back up and drive home this comment: "Broken fellowship, lost usefulness, and open rebellion all depict the perishing condition of an individual without Christ." People in each of those three lifestyles are probably sitting in the congregation. The concluding paragraph uses personal pronouns to apply the need for personal choice to the listeners. The invitation can do even more.

REACTION AND RESPONSE

Seek help on evangelistic preaching from Ken Hemphill, "Preaching and Evangelism," *Handbook of Contemporary Preaching*, (Nashville: Broadman and Holman, 1992) 518–528.

Chapter 20
Doctrinal Preaching

Timothy was reminded that "all Scripture is given by inspiration of God and is profitable for doctrine, for reproof, for correction, for instruction in righteousness" (2 Tim. 3:16). Doctrinal sermons help Christians to be "thoroughly equipped for every good work." The doctrinal sermon has as its objective the explanation of a specific Bible doctrine. All biblical sermons contain doctrine or teaching, but a doctrinal sermon explains a specific Scripture doctrine. The first Christians heard doctrinal sermons as evidenced by Acts 2:42, "They continued steadfastly in the apostles' doctrine." Preaching doctrinal sermons fulfills Jesus' instructions to teach "them to observe all things I have commanded you" (Matt. 28:20). Paul encouraged Timothy to "give attention . . . to doctrine. Take heed to yourself and to the doctrine. Continue in them" (1 Tim. 4:13, 16). Doctrinal sermons are more difficult to prepare than other kinds of sermons. Persevere in them; your church will be stronger.

Timothy George observed, "The very word doctrine, like its cousins dogma and dogmatic, has fallen on hard times. For many people it connotes authoritarianism, intellectualism, and legalism. When applied to preaching it comes out rigid and stultifying, rather than dynamic and edifying."[1] Your job as a preacher is to prevent that from happening. Many doctrinal sermons are topical and share the primary weakness of that kind of preaching—too broad a subject. Limit the subject of the doctrinal sermon to one part of the doctrine. Andrew Blackwood suggested, "no sermon should try to explain everything about a doctrine. Don't try to play God when you preach doctrine."[2]

Most Bible doctrines involve many related subjects. This chart lists some suggestions for topics of basic Bible doctrines.

Doctrinal Preaching

Doctrine of God
- The Trinity
- The Love of God
- God's Sovereignty
- The Grace of God
- God, The Creator
- The Wrath of God
- The Providence of God
- God, The Father

Doctrine of Jesus Christ
- Jesus, The Messiah
- The Virgin Birth
- Jesus' Resurrection
- Christ, Our Mediator
- Jesus, Son of Man
- The Suffering Servant
- The Ascended Christ
- The Lordship of Christ
- Jesus' Divine Nature
- Jesus' Human Nature

Doctrine of the Holy Spirit
- The Counselor
- The Spirit Filled Christian
- Grieving the Holy Spirit
- Spiritual Gifts
- The Spirit in Evangelism
- The Spirit in Missions

Doctrine of the Bible
- Inspiration of the Scriptures
- The Unity of the Book
- The Bible, Our Authority
- The Word of Promise

Doctrine of Man
- Free Will of Man
- The Unpardonable Sin
- The Privilege of Prayer
- All Have Sinned
- Priesthood of Believers

Doctrine of the Church
- The Foundation of the Church
- The Unity of the Church
- Church Ordinances
- The Nature of the Church
- The Church and Missions
- Church Leadership

Doctrine of Salvation
- At One with God
- Confess and Be Saved
- The Righteousness of Christ
- Am I Sanctified?
- Conviction of Sin
- Converted to Life
- Who Are the Elect?
- Glorified in Glory

Doctrine of Last Things
- Why Do We Die?
- Christ's Second Coming
- Judgment Is Coming
- When We All Get To Heaven
- The Resurrected Body
- Christ's Rule on the Earth
- Where is the Kingdom?
- Is Hell Real?

Other Doctrines
- The Christian and Government
- What About Angels?
- Religous Liberty
- Satan, The Deceiver

Each of the ideas listed above can be limited further, and in most cases should be. The doctrine of prayer has many possibilities for doctrinal sermons, as suggested by these ideas:

Prayer and the Will of God	Pray in Faith
Hindrances to Prayer	Intercessory Prayer
The Lord's Prayer	Prayer for the Lord's Laborers

The more specific you make a doctrinal sermon, the stronger it will be.

The providence of God is a basic doctrine found throughout the Bible. A sermon on the entire subject would be difficult to prepare and preach, and probably too long for most to hear. The following student-sermon outline limits the doctrine to God's providential work as seen in Paul's life. The message was preached to a pastor's conference and contained relevant illustrations from a pastor's life.

Acts of Providence for Christian Workers
God's work of providence can be seen in Paul's life and in ours.
  I. In the work of conversion (Acts 9:1–4; 22:1–21).
  II. In providing ministry needs (Acts 18:1–4; 28:7).
  III. In answered prayer (Acts 16:25; 28:8).
  IV. In directing the course of ministry (Acts 13:46–47).
  V. In preserving us from evil (Acts 9:23–25; 18:12–15; 25:3–4).

A more appealing title might be, "A Providential Ministry." The people might become lost in the many references. The sermon could be tighter by an arrangement that moved from the earlier chapters of Acts to the later references. Point IV would fit better as point II. It is also possible to omit the point on prayer and include it within the other areas. "Pray for ministry needs and trust God's providence to provide," or "Pray for God to direct the course of your ministry and trust His providence to do it best." This sermon demonstrates an effective way to preach doctrine. Show how the truth comes about in the life of the believer. Relevant application to the lives of people keeps the message from becoming a lecture on systematic theology. Theology is best communicated in the classroom when it is accompanied by life application.

Relate the doctrine to life. A doctrinal sermon should not be a theological lecture. Blackwood observed, "The ultimate purpose of doctrine is a changed life. The doctrine preached should have a bearing on human need."[3] In the above sermon outline on God's providence, the application to Christian

Doctrinal Preaching

workers was made throughout the sermon. The introduction included a quotation from missionary David Livingston's diary, followed by this sentence: "He believed in the doctrine of the providence of God. You and I, to be successful in ministry, need to believe it too." Jay Adams, commenting on the doctrine of Philippians 2, said, "doctrinal truth should be preached as practical truth and forcefully applied to people who divisively put themselves and their own interests first in the congregation. He [Paul] wanted doctrine to humble, shame, and guide them, bringing them to repentance and newness of life in Christ."[4]

In the preceding chapter on evangelistic preaching the sermon on John 3:16 was doctrinal with an evangelistic goal. Doctrinal preaching will never be "dry" when the truth relates to basic life needs.

Biblical teaching on death is the theme of the following message. The simple outline is rich in truth. It is an example of an expository-doctrinal sermon with a strong pastoral purpose. The message encourages believers as they face death.

Death Be Not Proud (Rev. 1:17–20)[5]

In Revelation, John gives three reasons why death can no longer be proud and arrogant toward those who are trusting Jesus.

I. Jesus has fully experienced death (vv. 17–18).

All of death's mysteries have been explored and revealed by Jesus.

II. Jesus has completely conquered death (v. 18).

"I am the living one." In his resurrection Jesus conquered death.

III. Jesus has total control of death (v. 18).

Jesus has the keys to death and the grave in his hands! Satan no longer holds those keys. Satan no longer controls death and the grave. Jesus has conquered them both and has total control of them.

The title of this message came from a poem by English poet John Donne. John Gunther used the words to title his book, *Death Be Not Proud*, which tells the story of the last fifteen months his son, Johnny, lived. The sermon began with these words.

> He was a blond-haired, blue-eyed boy named Johnny. He never enjoyed many of the things that normal teenagers enjoy because Johnny died of a brain tumor when he was only seventeen.

The introduction begins where we all are. Most of us have experienced death striking down with seeming arrogance a young person with so much potential. Interest and relevance are immediately established. The introduction includes a few lines from Donne's poem which "picture death, conquered and humbled by Jesus Christ." The transition to the text and the first division reads: "In Revelation John gives three reasons why death can no longer be proud and arrogant toward those who are trusting in Jesus." Each transition includes the words from the title as this movement into the third division, "Finally, death can no longer be proud toward us because Jesus has total control of it." Each section of the text, supportive of the major division, is quoted immediately after the transition sentence. Throughout the sermon the congregation faces the Word of God. The message remains on the central theme of death conquered by Christ. Doctrine has been imparted through the elixir of hope.

Evidently this preacher's favorite source for illustrations is English literature, which contains rich material. In the conclusion two English writers are quoted and the last words are another poem. Variety with a more contemporary illustration would have strengthened the conclusion. He could have used the testimony of someone facing death now.

The doctrine of the church is the theme of a sermon by Alfred L. Miller.[6] Note his outline.

God's People in God's World (1 Pet. 1:22–2:12)
 I. We are God's people.
    We have been redeemed with the precious blood of Jesus.
 II. We are God's priests.
    Every child is meant to be a priest of God. We are the means of other people coming to know, love, and trust Jesus Christ.
 III. We are God's pilgrims.
    A pilgrim passes through. We are temporary residents with a purpose and a destination. On our journey toward heaven, we need a daily supply of food from God's Word (1 Pet. 2:2). We will need a generous supply of love for others (1 Pet. 1:22).

At the cross Jesus made us God's people, God's priests, and God's pilgrims. That's who we are. Isn't it time we lived like that?

The conclusion moves toward the purpose of the sermon which calls the church to deeper commitment to her purpose as God's people. The conclusion shows the results of the preacher's reading.

A World War I novel related the story of two young men who became inseparable companions. One was from a fine, outstanding family and had lived a decent and wholesome life. The other grew up on the wrong side of the tracks and had been in constant trouble.

An enemy bullet felled the young man from the fine family. As he lay dying in the arms of his friend, he said to him, "Your name has many marks against it. Give me your name, and let it die with me. You take my name and live a new life."

Jesus Christ did that, and more, for us. At the cross he took our names, our lives, and our sins, and let them die with him. He came forth from the tomb and gave us his name and a new life to live by his daily grace.

At the cross, Jesus made us God's people, God's priests, and God's pilgrims. That's who we are. Isn't it time we lived like it?

The church's purpose includes worship. Consider the outline of an expository sermon on Isaiah 6:1–8, which Edward D. Johnson prepared on the theme of worship.[7] The introduction includes this thesis sentence, "What really ought to happen when a person goes to church?" The text is introduced with this paragraph.

> Someone else has given a clear definition of worship. This young man, a true aristocrat from the ruling class of his day, gives us the best picture I have ever seen of what should happen when a person goes to church. His experience is recorded in the first eight verses of the sixth chapter of Isaiah.

Don't you find that more appealing than beginning, "My text today is from Isaiah 6?"

When a Person Goes to Church (Isa. 6:1–8)

Here is what Isaiah said should happen when a person goes to church.
  I. He should see the holiness of God (vv. 1–3)
  II. He should see his own true nature (v. 5).
  III. He should see the necessity and availability of cleansing (vv. 6–7).
  IV. He should see God's will for his life (v. 8).
  V. He should see his own level of commitment (vv. 8b-9a).

Notice how each division is stated in present tense. The structure follows the logical movement of the text.

Except for the sermon on God's providence as seen in the life of Paul, the sermon outlines found in this lesson demonstrate my favorite approach with doctrinal sermons. Locate a primary Scripture passage and preach an expository sermon with a doctrinal purpose. Other passages can be brought in as support material. Quote these or refer to them without having the people turn to them. Focusing on one passage helps limit the message and usually provides enough material for a full message.

As a pastor, plan to preach doctrinal sermons at various times during the year. The members of your church need to know what they believe and develop resources to explain their faith to others. Many sects are growing by getting members from our churches who do not know what they believe.

REACTION AND RESPONSE

Study Timothy George, "Doctrinal Preaching," by in *Handbook of Contemporary Preaching,* 93–102.

Chapter 21
Ethical Preaching

Ethical sermons apply biblical teachings to morality and daily life. This type of sermon asks or urges people to "think, act, and live" by Bible teachings. Ethical sermons rebuke, correct, and train the believer in righteous living. Some ethical issues include sexuality, divorce, stealing, drug abuse, abortion, citizenship, race relations, war, peace, church-state relations, health, economic injustice, and work. Biblical principles help guide Christians in making decisions about these areas of daily life.

Christian ethics (knowing what is right to do) comes from the gospels and the epistles. The power to do right comes from the Holy Spirit living within the believer. Good living (ethics) results from being born again. A Christian's ethics come as a result of his relationship with Jesus. Ethics must not substitute for evangelism, but neither must evangelism be divorced from ethics. The Apostle Peter asked, "What manner of persons ought you to be?" (2 Pet. 3:11). Ethical sermons give biblical principles for a godly life.

ETHICAL SERMONS WITH AN EDGE

When we preach ethical sermons, the message ought to have the quality of "the two-edged sword." The message must move beyond traditional slogans to find what the Lord says and convince those who hear His word to do something about it. The beginning of that process comes when we let the Bible speak for itself. Personal prejudices have dictated many so-called ethical sermons. The end result condoned prevailing practices rather than confronted them with the judgment of God. Let the Scripture direct the content of your ethical sermons. For centuries, race segregation was supported by a false Bible interpretation. Some said the mark on Cain was the color of his skin. Does the Bible say what the mark was? Genesis 4:15 remains silent on that point. Let the Bible speak for itself.

Ethical sermons are strongest when they emphasize major issues. Timothy was told to have nothing to do with "foolish and ignorant disputes, knowing that they generate strife" (2 Tim. 2:23). Issues which do not affect salvation and Christian growth deserve less emphasis. Ethics should not become a whip you use against changing fashion styles or length of hair. Paul showed selective use of words and stressed abiding principles when he wrote about women's appearance (1 Tim. 2:9–10).

A positive message produces more fruit than a negative whipping. A preacher with strong feelings on an ethical issue must not argue or become hostile and uncooperative. "Preaching out of anger may feel good at the time, especially when we've built up a good head of steam. But in the long run it doesn't accomplish what we're after."[1] Timothy was reminded to "convince, rebuke, and exhort with all longsuffering and teaching . . . be watchful in all things" (2 Tim. 4:2, 5). Condemnation of the wrong will prove ineffective without encouragement to do the right.

Secure factual information and know what you are talking about. I remember a pastor being quite upset about a movie which he felt "blasphemed Christ." He wanted the editor of the state Baptist paper to write an editorial condemning the film and help support a boycott of it. The editor asked me and two other pastors to view the film. We found it to be a rather funny satire on false messiahs and unworthy of major attention which would probably give it more support. I even used it as a sermon illustration. Had I launched into it on another's word, a more thoughtful member would have realized I did not know what I was talking about and questioned my judgment on other issues.

Pastoral sensitivity for hurting people flows through authentic ethical preaching. My awareness and understanding of the AIDS problem took on a new dimension when the hemophiliac son of a member became infected as a result of a contaminated blood transfusion. I've noticed many pastors are more sensitive toward the pain and trauma of the divorced after a member of their own family has experienced it. Many Christians have to go through decisions forced upon them by the wrong of others. Can they find comfort and encouragement from the shepherd of Christ, even while they hear the high standard of the Lord?

Ethical Preaching

Keep the message practical. Relate the doctrine to situations people face in daily life. Practical suggestions and everyday illustrations will help. Ethical theory will not be received well. I heard a sermon entitled "The Moral Dilemma in America," based on Psalm 119:49, 123, 137–144. The introduction indicated the message would deal with "four major value systems in the USA and how God feels about each." The first three were introduced with these headings: "Socio-biological View," "Situational Ethics," "Scientific Cultural Relativism." The fourth view was introduced with these sentences: "Morality can never be based on behavior, situations, or culture. The only good standard is the Bible, and Psalm 119 tells us why." His first three sections needed to be that plain. Why not describe the three systems in everyday terms, such as, "Why do people act the way they do?" or better, "Why do we act the way we do?" We explain our actions in one of three ways: (1) "I can't help it; I was born this way"; (2) "The situation determines my decision"; and (3) "Everyone else is doing it."

Lamar E. Cooper prepared a sermon on the sanctity of life using the primary text of Exodus 20:13.[2] Let's look at the outline of this example of ethical preaching.

The Principle of Life (Exod. 20:13)

We may be living in the most violent period of human history. (The introduction cites several statistics on crime, assisted suicide, and abortion.) These grim facts underscore the little value that is placed on human life today.

   I. Human life is sacred.

   II. Human life is a sacred trust to the individual.

   III. Human life is the sacred trust of the community.

Clarity and smoother transition come with full sentence outlining, as this sermon demonstrates. Each division relates to the main theme—the sanctity of life. The primary text is used throughout the message but the message also cites Genesis 1–3; Jeremiah 1:5; 1 Corinthians 15; Psalm 139:13–14; 1 Corinthians 6:19; Matthew 5:21–22; and several Old Testament passages in support of the third division. The printed version of this message may have included more Scripture than actually used. With this much material the preacher can refer to selected passages rather than have the congregation turn to each reference. Of course, the message carries more authority if key passages are examined in more detail.

The Labor Day holiday provides an opportunity to preach an ethical sermon on work relationships.

Why Do You Work? (Gen. 1:26–31; Eph. 4:28)
I. We work to cooperate with God in subduing the world (Gen. 1:26–31).
  A. Work fulfills God's command (Ex. 10:9).
  B. Honest work cooperates with God (Eph. 4:28; James 5:1–6).
II. We work to have something to share (Eph. 4:28).
  A. Work enables us to participate in giving to the less fortunate (Acts 20:35).
  B. We can give to share the gospel and build up the church.

Notice how the unity of this message is maintained by using the key word "work" in every transition. A question-to-answer format provides the basic structure. Application can be made by asking pertinent questions such as "Does your work glorify God?" "Do our work relationships display our true relationship to God?" "Are you using the resources of your work to help the less fortunate—homeless, aged, one-parent children?" Some use work as an excuse to stay away from church. "I work six days a week; Sunday is my only day off."

Race relations is an ethical issue affecting everyone. God can use you in relating the Scripture to improving relations between races. This sermon used the words of a popular song for the title and to introduce the theme. My son has remembered this sermon more than any other because of the title. The message was based on the meeting between Peter (Jew) and Cornelius (Gentile). The text involves several ideas, including missions, but this sermon chose the theme of prejudice. Relevant application can be made throughout the sermon. Current news stories chronicle racial divisions, and most communities have evidence of prejudice. A testimony of how God changed an individual's attitude, or the results which came from getting to know a person of another race, could illustrate the second point.

Ebony and Ivory (Acts 10:1–20)
"Ebony and ivory living in perfect harmony side by side on my piano keyboard. Oh, Lord, why don't we?"
I. Divisions mark our world.
  Peter and Cornelius illustrate racial divisions and racial prejudice in our world. Jews referred to Gentiles as dogs and supported their prejudice as a principle of their faith.
II. It is possible for the divisions to fall.
  A. God works with individuals to overcome prejudice. In worship and prayer, God spoke to Cornelius (vv. 1–8). God changed Peter's attitude through a vision (vv. 9–14).
  B. Individuals were obedient to God's leadership (vv. 9–8, 19–23).

Ethical Preaching

    C. Hospitality helped overcome prejudice (v. 24). Prejudice begins to fall when strangers become friends.
    D. God's word took priority over human tradition (v. 28).
III. Christ overcomes the divisions and unites us (vv. 36–41).
    Jesus, Lord of all, is the way to perfect harmony among people. This "good news" is available to everyone. The Spirit within produces the fruit of love. Jesus breaks down the dividing walls and makes one new person (Eph. 2:14).

Citizenship is always a relevant subject for ethical sermons. Independence Day and other civil holidays are opportunities for messages that explain Bible teachings on Christian citizenship and call Christians to be responsible citizens. Both Peter and Paul wrote on this subject. They have similar ideas, but messages can be prepared with different perspectives. These two expository sermon outlines look at citizenship first from the responsibility of the citizen and then the responsibility of the government. The first sermon would gain a better hearing the week before federal income taxes are due. The title and outline could be restructured to fit an opening illustration on paying taxes. We owe the government more than taxes. We owe submission, a good life, the practice of our freedom, respect, and honor.

A Christian Response to the Government (1 Pet. 2:13–17)

The Apostle Peter wrote this letter to encourage Christians who faced persecution. They lived under a dictatorial government. What is his advice to Christians on how to respond to government?

  I. A Christian submits to the government (vv. 13–14).
    Submission is for "the Lord's sake." Governments are "sent by Him."
 II. A Christian should do good (vv. 14–15).
    Government exists to punish wrong and commend good. Doing good is God's will and results in orderly society.
III. A Christian should live freely (v. 16).
    Use the freedom God gives; live the freedom of God's servant.
IV. A Christian must give respect and honor (v. 17).
    Respect the governing authorities; honor the king (president).

The Responsibility of Government (Rom. 13:1–7)

Governments exist all over the world. Sometimes we don't like what government does. As a citizen we have the right to express our opinions; as a Christian we have the responsibility to support the government. Government leaders and Christians both should be aware of the Bible's teaching on the responsibility of government.

I. Governing authorities are responsible to God (vv. 1–2).
God created the institution of government to give order to the world of relationships. All authorities are accountable to God.
II. Governing authorities are responsible to do right (vv. 3–5).
The assignment given to authorities by God is to develop good and discourage evil. Governments who perform evil will face God's wrath.
III. Governing authorities are responsible to the people (vv. 6–7).
People give taxes, honor, support in order for the powers to govern. The rulers are to be worthy of the honor and responsible with the use of taxes.

Both of the above sermons use a key word in the title and each major division. The outlines flow naturally from the text. Examples of Christian government officials and responsible citizenship can add relevance to both messages. The response might involve asking Christian leaders to share in a commitment time at the close of the message. They could kneel for prayer, and the people could join them in seeking God's will for responsible leadership.

Christians need to know how their beliefs apply to life. An ethical sermon fulfills this purpose and applies Bible teachings to morality and daily living. The desired result is that people "think, act, and live" by Bible teachings. Ethical issues will constantly surface in your community. Turn the light of the Bible on these issues and help your people make decisions on how to live.

REACTION AND RESPONSE

Read "Dealing with Controversial Subjects" Hybels, Briscoe, and Robinson, *Mastering Contemporary Preaching*, 79–86.

Chapter 22
Pastoral Preaching

Hurting people sit before us when we stand to preach. Memories of these, among many others from congregations I served, still linger in my mind.

- A college student comes home and tells his parents about his homosexual lifestyle.
- A father with teenagers is diagnosed with Alzheimer's disease.
- Retirement starts this week for a successful executive.
- A hemophiliac son copes with AIDS contracted from a blood transfusion.
- A young woman without children faces a hysterectomy on Tuesday.
- A twenty-eight-year marriage appears headed for divorce.
- A couple grieves the loss of their daughter, killed by a drunk driver.
- Depression completely debilitates a promising professional.

A steady diet of evangelistic preaching will not help these hurting people. Pastoral sermons are needed to minister to people in crises and suffering. They offer biblical guidance and impart hope, comfort, and encouragement.

Pastors struggle with priorities of preaching and pastoral care. The two complement each other rather than compete. Franklin Segler wrote, "Ideally, preaching and the care of souls are the major functions of the pastoral office."[1]

Harry M. Fosdick defined preaching as "pastoral counseling on a group basis—nothing else." He was noted for sermons that started with "a life issue, a real problem."

I found that within a paragraph or two after the sermon started, first one listener and then another would discover that the preacher was bowling down his alley, and sometimes the whole congregation would grow tense and quiet, seeing that the sermon concerned a matter of vital import to everyone of them.[2]

The church is a flock shepherded by the Lord God. Isaiah balanced his presentation of the Sovereign Lord of power with this tender portrait:

He will feed his flock like a shepherd:
He will gather the lambs with his arms
and carry them in his bosom;
and gently lead those who are with young. (40:11)

Jesus called Himself the Good Shepherd (John 10). Peter, remembering the Lord's teaching, called the church a flock that needed protection and love (Acts 20:28–29; 1 Pet. 5:1–4). While eating breakfast in a restaurant, I overheard two men in an adjoining booth discussing the new pastor they anticipated for their church. One man stated the essential quality, "I just want him to love us." Authentic pastoral preaching comes from a shepherd-pastor and communicates love for the flock entrusted to him by the Lord.

GRACE TO STAND DURING STRESS

A stress test[3] lists forty-three sources of stress with each stress assigned points indicating the level of intensity. The top twenty situations and stress points are the following:

1. Death of spouse	100
2. Divorce	73
3. Marital separation from mate	65
4. Detention in jail or other institution	63
5. Death of a close family member	63
6. Major personal injury or illness	53
7. Marriage	50
8. Being fired at work	47
9. Marital reconciliation with mate	45
10. Retirement from work	45
11. Major change in health/behavior of a family member	44
12. Pregnancy	40

13. Sexual difficulties	39
14. A new family member (birth, adoption, parent)	39
15. Major business adjustment	39
16. Major change in financial state (better or worse)	38
17. Death of a close friend	37
18. Changing to a different line of work	36
19. Major change in number of arguments with spouse	35
20. Taking on a mortgage greater than $10,000	31

These twenty stresses can be grouped into four categories: death, family, health, and work/finances. Of course, work and health problems impact family life, and death affects the other three. All these stresses involve interpersonal relationships. Your preaching should include messages to help people cope with these stresses.

Our own personal struggles with life are a source for pastoral sermons. As Harold T. Bryson noted, "Confessional preaching is the way you began to preach."[4] We were converted and began to tell others about that life-changing experience. Others are trying to cope with situations you have probably faced:

- How to honor parents when their values clash with yours
- Releasing a child to school or marriage
- A co-worker who refuses to forgive
- A grandparent dies
- Relocation
- Hospitalization and surgery
- Depression
- Loneliness
- Your anger got out of control
- Dealing with divorce in the family

Accepting your own limitations and needs and honestly evaluating how those are met will generate sensitive pastoral messages.

Clyde Fant observed that Paul's confession at Lyconia, "We are men like yourselves . . ." (Acts 14:15), is the second greatest confession of the early church. "Unfortunately, most of life is spent either in the postponement of this confession or in the self-deception that it is not true. Nothing could be more destructive to Christian ministry."[5] This acknowledgement of our humanity enables us to be used by God to truly make the Word flesh. The strongest pastoral preaching reflects the preacher's humanity, and better reception comes because people are aware you've been in the situation and honestly faced it with God's grace.

The scarcity of pastoral preaching in some churches may come from the wrong interpretation of Acts 6:4, the selection of deacons. "We will turn this responsibility over to them and will give our attention to prayer and the ministry of the Word" (NIV). Some preachers just want to pray, study, and preach. Visitation and personal relationship building are left to others. Seek a balance between preparation and pastoral work. They feed each other. Often I have been stymied in the study but, after visitation, found new light and insight for the message.

With little contact with the people, a preacher will seem aloof, remote, and uninterested in the people. Consequently, the people will be less interested in the preaching. Become aware of the people's work and family needs. Relate to them on their turf. Home visitation, hospital calls, availability in crisis and joyful transition times will make the preacher aware of many people needs and provide material for pastoral preaching.

Community resources increase awareness of people needs. Visit law enforcement officials and social service leaders to discover community needs. Census statistics reveal much data on a community and describe transitions which create stress. How are the people handling a factory closing? What impact does farm losses have on your rural community? Think about the emotions and stress in a community when the local army reserve was activated during the Persian Gulf crisis.

The study will generate other ideas for pastoral preaching. Probe for people needs as you study the Bible. Any passage including relationships has potential for pastoral preaching. Elijah's depression, Peter's guilt, Job's suffering, Saul's jealousy, David's grief, and Mary's pregnancy mirror a few of the needs in any congregation.

A varied reading program adds additional sermon ideas and illustrative material for pastoral preaching. A basic understanding of psychological needs is required for pastoral preaching. An awareness of life needs of various age groups will make your sermons more relevant.

RISKS IN PASTORAL PREACHING

Pastoral preaching involves some risks to which the preacher must remain alert. Helpful pastoral preaching encourages people to seek help and often they will seek the pastor and church. Are you prepared to counsel? Are more qualified counselors available and will you refer? Are support groups in the church? Could your church join others and open a Christian counseling

Pastoral Preaching

center? Increased frustration and disappointment come when pastoral preaching is not coupled with personalized pastoral care.

A big risk comes from the temptation of diverting your priority from preaching to counseling. Each pastor will do some counseling, but the church only has one whom the Lord has called to "preach the Word" week by week as the undershepherd of the flock. Protect your preparation time and refuse to become involved in prolonged counseling with an individual. Develop other resources and be quick to refer.

Lloyd Perry[6] suggested some other dangers:

- the violation of confidence
- handling (the problem) inadequately
- substituting psychology for Christianity
- allowing biblical content to be crowded out of the sermon
- confusing Christian morality with natural virtue
- the preacher's message being dictated by some emotional need of his own demanding satisfaction

PREPARING THE PASTORAL SERMON

I have tried to emphasize in other places within this text the need to maintain balance between understanding the text and application to life. The pastoral sermon especially demands this. The message needs to be alive with relevance, with the congregation feeling as if they are walking through a problem, out into the light, with the pastor.

Philippians 3:12–14 is the text for a sermon entitled "You Can Live Beyond Yourself!"[7] The message begins with these questions: "Do you ever feel boxed in? Do you ever have the feeling that life is passing you by?" The transition to the first division uses the sermon title and connects with comments already made about the text: "You can live beyond yourself! Paul outlines four steps for this kind of creative living." The message included these four steps:

1. Face up to the fact you are not perfect (v.12).
2. Live with your back to the past (v. 13b).
3. Keep your eye on the right goal (v. 14).
4. Go for broke—"I press on." (v. 13).

The message uses plenty of personal pronouns, always linking Paul's experience with the contemporary. Imaginative language helps visualize the issues.

"Some of us lean continually on glass crutches made out of our own achievements. Do you carry the garbage out in Hefty bags? Some of us carry Hefty bags over our shoulders all through life. Every day we put them down, and we put in a bit more garbage. Then we lift them up over our shoulders again. That's not living beyond ourselves." Variety in illustrative material includes biblical background material, quotation from a psychiatrist, comments made by a former business colleague, quote from a poet, a story from a novel, the philosophy of an actress, a discus thrower in action.

The following message, "Christian Forgiveness,"[8] is an excellent example of an expository sermon with pastoral emphases. Strong illustrations introduce and conclude the message. The alliterated structure reflects an unforced, natural choice of words. The sermon is the product of extensive study of words and context. Four other Scripture references support the primary text. I repeat an earlier word of caution about the use of Greek terms. The shift in pronouns in verse 13 could be noted without the use of "reciprocal/reflexive" terminology. Additional application of specific ideas would increase the relevance to an individual's life. The broad title sounds like a doctrinal paper. A more appealing title, found in the sermon, is "A Heart for Forgiveness."

CHRISTIAN FORGIVENESS (Col. 3:12-15)

Just before Leonardo Da Vinci began his most famous painting, *The Last Supper* he had a violent argument with another painter. Too proud to seek forgiveness, both left the encounter in a storm of rage. When Leonardo sat down to paint he was still so angry that he began to plot revenge, and quickly devised the perfect scheme. He painted the face of Judas Iscariot, the infamous betrayer of Christ, as the face of the other painter. In his anger his painting was fast and frantic. Da Vinci's powerful memory recaptured every detail of his enemy's face as the face of Judas. But, when Leonardo attempted to paint the face of Christ, it seemed some invisible hand restrained his own, a mental block that prevented him from envisioning and portraying the likeness of Christ. He threw down his brush in frustration and, after some thought, concluded that what hindered him from being able to envision and capture the image of Christ was his vengeful act of painting the face of Judas to resemble his enemy. In a silent act of forgiveness, he wiped out the face of Judas and began to paint, freely and unhindered now, the face of Christ that is recognized today as one of the greatest masterpieces of all time.

What is the lesson of this story? A person cannot envision and portray the image of Christ without a heart for forgiveness. Colossians 3:12–15 tells us how to obtain this forgiving heart. Verse 10 states the believer is a new person being renewed in the image of his Creator, Jesus Christ. One of the primary characteristics of Christ is gracious forgiveness. Our transformation will never approach completion until we are willing to forgive others as Christ has forgiven us. To manifest the image of Christ, our lives must be characterized by a willingness to forgive others.

The power for forgiveness comes from our identity in Christ. In verse 12 Paul reminds us again we are God's chosen people. A fundamental principle of Old Testament religion was that the people of God were to manifest the character of God. The fundamental attribute of God's character is holiness. Divine attributes of love, righteousness, purity, and justice, are offshoots of this central characteristic. God told the Old Testament saints, "Be ye therefore holy for I am holy." When the people of God manifest the character of God, forgiving others becomes natural and spontaneous, the almost automatic expression of their new nature. Perhaps the Colossians argued that their harsh intolerance of sin, their cold legalism, and their judgmental attitudes expressed God's holiness. Paul explains that genuine holiness produces the very opposite kind of character. Holiness is not an excuse to refuse to forgive others; it is the incentive for forgiving others.

First, God's holiness expresses itself in compassion. We could translate the Greek, "Bowels of mercy," as "gutwrenching love." The term describes that empathy we feel for someone when we look upon his or her agony and somehow share in it. This is the compassion of Christ for people as sheep without a shepherd, for those staggering with hunger, for the lepers in their pain. Christ loves us in this deep, stirring way, and expresses his compassion through gracious forgiveness. As partakers of his character, we should love others and express that love through forgiveness.

Second, God's holiness expresses itself in kindness, the character quality that leads one to treat others graciously though they mistreat him. In Romans 2:4 it describes the character of God who blesses those who despise Him in order to lead them to repentance. The Sermon on the Mount describes the kindness that turns the other cheek and goes the second mile.

Third, God's holiness expresses itself in humility. How can God's character be described as "humble?" Philippians 2:5 states, "Your attitude should be the same as that of Christ Jesus; Who . . . humbled himself, and became obedient to death—even death on a cross." Loving and forgiving sinners was a very humbling thing for God. It required him to leave heaven's throne and be born in a stable, laid in a feed trough, wrapped in rags, rejected, scorned, and crucified. Loving and forgiving can be humbling for us today. It may demand that we swallow our pride and abandon our personal rights. It may mean that we look like spineless cowards or groveling idiots to others. But humility expresses holiness, and is an essential characteristic of the image of God, and a motivation for forgiveness.

Fourth, God's holiness expresses itself in gentleness. The Greek word is "meekness," the ability to gracefully endure the abuses of others. I earlier defined "kindness" as the ability to treat others well though they mistreat you. But it is possible to treat them well to their faces, then get away from them to fume and fuss. But meekness so gracefully endures the abuses of others that there is no hidden masked resentment. Numbers 12:3 describes Moses as "more meek than anyone else on the face of the earth." Why is Moses so described? In that passage, Miriam and Aaron, Moses' brother and sister, began to spread rumors about their brother and undermine his authority. They were angry with him for marrying a Cushite, a black woman. As punishment for undermining the authority of their spiritual leader, God struck Miriam with leprosy. Now if many of us had been Moses we would have shouted, "Alright, get'um God. Let'um have it!" But not Moses. Verse 13 says, "Moses cried out to the LORD, "O God please heal her." Meekness drives you to your knees to plead for God to bless those who abuse you, even in private.

Fifth, God's holiness expresses itself in patience. Patience is the ability to endure the abuses of others without losing your cool or letting your emotions get away from you.

A claim to personal and divine holiness is no excuse to refuse to forgive; the holiness of God compels you to forgive and grants you the spiritual character that empowers you to forgive.

The text also shows us the **principles for forgiveness** First, remember that the offences of others against us are small in comparison to our offences against God. What is it that the Colossians are to forgive? Grievances. In Greek, the word means, "complaint" or "gripe." The New Testament usually uses strong words for the abuses of others that are to be forgiven, words like offence, debt, sins, insult, and evil. The word "complaint" or "gripe" seems to be a conscious attempt by Paul to minimize, almost ridicule, the matters that divided people in the Colossian church. Unimportant, silly, and trifling matters separated them, and their conduct was childish.

God's Word urges us to see the sins of others against us in light of our sins against God. Think for a moment of the very worst sin that someone (particularly another Christian since Paul is speaking of Christians here) ever committed against you. It may seem so horrible; it may seem like the worst thing possible. But then remember that our sins against God spit in the face of divine authority, rejected and ridiculed his beloved Son, and ultimately nailed him to the cross. Suddenly the sins of others against us are dwarfed in size, trifling, unimportant, and can be more readily forgiven.

A second principle to remember is your special unity with other believers. In verse 13 Paul makes an important shift in pronouns, moving from a reciprocal pronoun "each other" to a reflexive pronoun "yourselves." So that verse 13 literally means "Bear with each other and forgive **yourselves.**" Is Paul saying that we have to forgive ourselves for the sins of our own individual past? No. This shift of pronouns stresses the corporate unity, the special togetherness of the church. Verse 15 states that members of the church have become one body. Because of our oneness with other Christians, forgiveness should be all the more simple.

Who is the easiest person in the world to forgive? Yourself. Many of us bow our heads at night to confess the sins of the day and sometimes can't think of any! It's not that we didn't commit them. We just forgot them all. But chances are you can remember every single detail about how someone mistreated you years and years ago. It is easier to forgive ourselves than others. Paul says that believers have been made one in Christ, forgiving them is like forgiving yourselves. Forgiving others should and can be done just as easily, just as readily, as we forgive ourselves.

The pattern for forgiveness is Christ's forgiveness of us. "Forgive just as the Lord forgave you." The comparative particle is intensive. It means we are to forgive others with the same kind, manner, and degree of forgiveness that Christ has extended to us.

Notice the breadth of forgiveness that Christ offers. Colossians 2:13 describes in detail the kind, manner, and degree of forgiveness Christ offers. He forgave all our sins, not just the little ones. He didn't just forgive the sins of our distant past. He forgave them all. Two definitions help us understand the depth of forgiveness Christ offers. First remember that the written code means "a certificate of indebtedness." It was a list of sins we committed against God and the punishment we deserved for those sins. Second, remember that the word cancel means to erase. First century writing materials were very expensive, and the ancients learned to sponge or scrape the ink off of papyri so thoroughly that no trace of it could be seen and the paper could be used again. A debt was normally not canceled by erasure as Paul describes here. The normal way was to mark a large Greek letter Chi through the document, to "X" it out. However when a certificate of debt was "Xed" out, the written record was still clearly visible—there for all to see. Paul's intense metaphor states that Christ didn't merely "X" out our sins; he completely erased them so that no trace of them remains.

Our forgiveness must be like that of Christ's; it should completely wipe out any trace of any memory of the evils done against us. 1 Corinthians 13 tells us that love does not keep a list of wrongs. The Jews believed in keeping lists. Thus the disciples asked Jesus, "Should I forgive my brother seven times." They would keep a list of sins, forgiving but also remembering. When the count reached seven, forgiveness stopped. The "forgiver" unleashed his fury for all the accumulated wrongs. True forgiveness doesn't keep lists. It erases lists. It doesn't keep count of sins. When one forgives, the sin is erased. The forgiver makes a conscious decision to relate to the offender just as if the offense had not occurred, never to be dredged up or mentioned again.

On Tuesday November 25, 1986, forty-seven-year-old Southern Baptist missionary Libby Senter and her ten-year-old daughter Rachel enjoyed the moments of sunset outside of their home in Yekepa, Liberia, catching bugs for their household lizard that had become something of a pet. Later they went inside so Libby could study her Bible and prepare for the next day's work. When Benjamin Morris appeared at the door of missionary George Senter's house, neither Mrs. Senter nor her daughter were surprised. He had been at the Senter home many times. Ben was a graduate of the Theological Seminary in Liberia but had not been able to keep a church. That very morning he had done work in the Senter home, unneeded odd jobs to make money to support himself. That evening when he knocked at the Senter's door, even though George was gone for the night, they had no hesitation about allowing a trusted friend to enter. But before the events of that dark night had passed, that trusted friend had brutally beaten and raped Rachel, then pulled a knife and murdered both mother and daughter. George, hundreds of miles away, received the message in gruesome detail over the radio and jumped in his four-wheel drive to make the long trek home. Morris had drunk a bottle of drain opener in an attempt to kill himself. The poison, not strong enough to kill him, did incapacitate him temporarily so that the police tracked him down. That morning over five hundred people lined the fences of the jail threatening to kill Morris on sight. When the missionary, George, went to speak with the police he knew that somehow he had to find it in his heart to face the man. Seated across from Morris, George was silent. His mind swept back to Rachel's goodnight hugs and warm laughter; his heart broken by the memories of his wife's tender touch and soothing voice. His mind was obsessed with the memory of the grizzly murder scene. As he saw the chemical burns from the poison on the murderer's mouth and chin, he found himself wishing that the poison had been stronger, wishing that Morris had died a slow and painful death. At just that moment something strange and unusual happened, something that George Senter does not fully understand even now. He looked into the eyes of his once trusted friend, put his hand on the man's shoulder and said, "Ben, God wants to forgive you if you'll let him. With God's help, I forgive you too."

The news of Senter's forgiveness appalled the nation even more than the murders themselves. Across the country, grudges that had been nursed for years were forgiven and forgotten. Broken churches were filled with new unity and harmony. A church in Nimba County that had split was reunited. One African woman approached her enemy and said, "This man has forgiven a man who wiped out his family. Surely we can forgive each other and patch up our differences." Men who had been bitter enemies for decades embraced. There was new power in the gospel that was preached across Liberia as people came to see the love of Christ in the heart of a Christian man who forgave the ultimate betrayal of one whom he regarded as a brother and a trusted friend. Christ was no longer an interesting character whose deeds were recorded in an ancient book. The people of Liberia saw Him in living color. Christ's character appeared in the face of one willing to erase the canvas, portray the image of Christ and forgive as Christ forgave. Will you manifest this image?

Time has not dated the vivid description Halford E. Luccock gave to preaching which seeks to meet human needs but becomes a weak substitute.
But with some preaching today, the psychological emphasis has been the camel in the tent, crowding into a corner or clearing out the rightful occupant. A continuous stream of sermons on how to be healthy, wealthy, and wise has kept people holding their own pulse and taking their temperature. The attention is too much centered on the audience, on themselves, while the high and holy object of religion—God—goes into a cloud. This modern Pilgrim's Progress is not a journey to the celestial City of God, beginning with a load

of sin falling from the back, and continuing in a life-and-death struggle with sin, but a pleasant little ramble to self-expression and success.[9]

People don't need pastoral preaching to make them feel better. Pastoral preaching should help them honestly face their hurts and experience God's sufficient grace.

Reaction and Response

Pastoral preaching seeks to understand the congregation and communicate the truth of God's Word. Consider suggestions found in Craig A. Loscalzo, *Preaching Sermons That Connect,* Intervarsity Press, 1992.

Unit 7

Making the Most of Preparation

By now you have surely realized preaching requires continuous preparation if you intend to preach as a workman who is not ashamed. With all the demands on a preaching minister's time, adequate preparation may seem an impossible mission. Develop ways to make the most of your preparation time. The following chapters highlight three areas which strengthen the preaching ministry.

A pastor's wife described their financial situation as "scraping by from one paycheck to the other." It turned out they exercised no control over their spending nor made any plans. A similar attitude prevails toward preaching. Preaching loses its joy when it becomes "scraping by from Sunday to Sunday." Planning a preaching schedule turns a preacher from "the weekly hunt" to creative study.

Few professionals prepare as much material for public presentation as does a preacher. The product of the study and the pulpit can be used again. Chapter 24 examines ways to "recycle" your messages. These additional uses expand the influence of the pulpit and add value to preparation time.

The continuing cost decline of computers and software now place these resources within reach of most preachers. Does a computer help? What are some available computer programs that make more use of preparation time? How can computer resources assist in preserving the work of your study time?

Chapter 23
Planning Your Preaching

Many major biblical events involve a myriad of details which need to mesh to fulfill God's plan. How would you have fared as foreman of the temple construction crew? Consider the planning involved in these events of biblical history:

- Noah building and loading the ark
- The Exodus from Egypt
- The building of the temple
- The missionary journeys of Paul

Our salvation was planned "from the creation of the world" (Rev. 13:8). Many preachers quickly point out the fulfillment of prophecy in Christ's coming, death, and resurrection, another way of noting God's plans were carried out. Isn't it ironic that some preachers deny chance rules their life but take that approach in preaching? Isn't it inconsistent to offer God's "plan of salvation," while claiming planned preaching is unspiritual?

Our daily life reflects a commitment to planning. Do we leave these events to chance, hoping they will fall in place at the right time: wedding ceremony, delivery of the baby, relocation to a new town, automobile maintenance, vacation? Life soon becomes chaotic without planning, and so does preaching. The issue becomes either good or bad planning, some planning or none.

Jesus encouraged planning in the parable of the tower builders (Luke 14:28). This parable "refutes the heresy that the Holy Spirit works best through those who plan least."[1]

SOME BENEFITS TO PLANNING

There are numerous benefits which come from a planned approach to preaching. The preacher's stress level immediately decreases with a preaching plan. Few things in the ministry are more frustrating than a frantic weekly search for an idea or a Scripture passage. As Sunday approaches, the stress builds and the need for a sermon may force a preacher to rely too much on another's material. Killinger noted, "The work of the Holy Spirit is not impeded by such planning; it is actually enhanced. When we are free from the anxiety of wondering what we shall preach from week to week, we can follow the Spirit's leading without constriction."[2]

Planning encourages variety by preventing an overemphasis on favorite Scriptures or themes. Sermon preparation which is left to the last moments usually takes the easiest and most familiar route. Every congregation appreciates a variety of themes or styles of delivery. Haddon Robinson observed, "Any preacher knows the weasel sameness that sucks life from a message. Perceptive preachers know that variety is not only the spice of life, but of preaching as well."[3] Varied congregational needs demand preaching variety, and this must be planned.

A preaching plan encourages a unified worship experience. Choir music, soloists, instrumental and hymn selections can be coordinated with the preaching theme.

Commitment to a preaching plan encourages disciplined study. Consistent reading and Bible study are essential to fill out planned messages with quality content. Announcing a plan places a burden of responsibility to prepare. The results are worth the discipline.

Preaching from a plan saves time. Background study for a series supports several sermons. Planned preaching allows more time to gather illustrative material. Life experiences and observations surface to support the messages. With the idea in mind, illustrations will be seen in the newspaper or in current events. The message will have more relevance. Delayed preparation relies more on material pulled from the memory, which the congregation has probably heard several times.

Planning helps the message mature. When preparation comes near the day for the message to be delivered, the message will not have had time to "ripen." We know people better the longer we live with them. Planning enables the preacher to live with the message longer and deliver it more from the heart. Raymond Calkins wrote, "Good sermons have a long history. They mature slowly. They are not made between Sundays. A week is too short a time for an idea to germinate, grow, blossom into full bloom."[4]

Planning Your Preaching

Phillip's translation of Ephesians 5:16 offers excellent advice for preaching: "Make the best use of your time, despite all the difficulties of these days." Through planning we make the best use of our time. Left unplanned, preaching suffers from insufficient study because "all the difficulties of these days" will take precedence.

TAKING TIME TO PLAN

Some of the best use of a preacher's time occurs in annual planning. Plan to plan. A pastor friend has agreement with his church that allows him at least one week, not considered as vacation time, each year for uninterrupted prayer, study, and planning for the next year. Normally, this can't occur in your normal routine. Withdraw as Jesus did to a quiet place. "If a minister can find some relatively secluded spot—far enough away from his church to keep his people from feeling that they can drive out to discuss matters with him, or that he can drive in for any celebration or difficulty that might arise—he has the makings of a good place to unpack the luggage of life and thought and get his planning done."[5]

J. Winston Pearce suggests the preacher "put in five hours of good work each morning" during the family vacation. Doing this early, while the family sleeps, will enable planning to occur "without too much self-righteousness!"[6] If you can't get away for planning time, include time to plan during a week when you are not scheduled to preach the following Sunday. Another alternative would block out some time each week until a preaching plan has been completed. Bi-vocational ministers may have to plan during a weekend or a series of evenings. Make planning a priority and find the time to complete the task.

If you have never planned your preaching, start with a three-month schedule. In the third month evaluate what you did and project a six-month schedule.

Pastor Bill Hybels has a three-step approach to sermon planning. The plan begins each April when nine members are asked to determine issues their friends face and suggest an ideal sermon series focused on these issues. These members can involve others and have thirty days to prepare a series title and emphasis. This group then takes a two-and-a-half day retreat to discuss the series ideas. From that session Hybels chooses twenty themes. Another group of church leaders and staff members decide which of these should receive priority during the coming year. "It's amazing to me the wealth of wisdom that comes out of a plurality of godly people who look at life differently than I do."[7]

A simple congregational survey, "Pastor, preach on this (problem or text)," provides direction for preaching plans. Determining congregational needs makes for more relevant preaching.

DECIDING ON A PLAN

After several years of primarily topical preaching or examining isolated texts I discovered the freedom of preaching "the Bible the way it was written, book by book, and, within each book, unit by unit."[8] A sermon series structured from a book of the Bible provides a basic approach to planning and a major section of a year's schedule. "How else can both pastor and people come to know the Bible so well?" Blackwood rhetorically asks.[9]

Ideally, a Bible book series needs to rest upon an intensive study started long before the series begins. Start the study by reading the Scripture several times. Note the logical divisions of the book and ideas that arise as you read. Determine the overall theme for the book and draft an initial outline. Background study on the historical, cultural, and literary setting will add other material. From this extensive study project a series. Begin more detailed study on the first section, maintaining a file on the series for materials you will garner that will be useful for later messages in the series. Harold Bryson's book, *Expository Preaching*, offers help for preaching through a book of the Bible.[10]

Preaching from books of the Bible builds your personal library in a systematic way. You will purchase helpful commentaries and other resource materials on the book.

Preaching through books of the Bible lets the Word of God come to the people as it develops from the text. If a passage zeroes in on a local problem, the preacher can't be charged with judging or ignoring the issue. During a series from Numbers, I was continually amazed at the relevance of the text to either a local or national issue.

Although some preachers have started at Genesis and continued through Revelation, most churches would probably appreciate variety. Blackwood suggested "40 percent from the Old Testament, 30 from the Gospels, and 30 from the remainder of the New Testament, with no free time for anything but biblical preaching."[11]

Some longer books such as Isaiah or the Psalms offer so much material you probably will want to divide the series and offer them between other material. Some books can be developed around major personalities. Genesis 12–50 chronicles God's work in the life of Abraham, Isaac, Jacob, and Joseph. The Gospel according to John offers a series of life-changing encounters between Jesus and individuals in need. One homiletics writer noted, "It is my feeling that we (pastors) are a lot more enamored with our series than our folks are."[12] Relevance to congregational need becomes a crucial factor in the value of a series.

Planning Your Preaching

Traditional approaches to planned preaching have utilized the Christian year, the national calendar, and the church or denominational calendar. A blending of these three easily fill a year with preaching ideas.

The Christian year includes seven seasons: Advent, Christmas, Epiphany, Lent, Easter, Pentecost, and Trinity. Old and New Testament Scriptures selected for each Sunday of the Christian year are gathered in a lectionary. The Christian Year schedule begins the Sunday nearest November 30. The seven seasons cover the entire span of God's work in the world and with the church. A preaching schedule which follows the Christian year provides a complete, balanced diet of biblical themes.

The national calendar prompts some preachers to plan sermons related to national holidays. These observances include New Year's Day, Martin Luther King Jr. Day, Mother's Day, Memorial Day, Father's Day, Independence Day, Election Day, Veterans Day, and Thanksgiving. Most of these days can be a starting point for preaching biblical texts on such issues and needs as racial prejudice, death, citizenship, home life, contentment, and commitment. The Sundays from Mother's Day through Father's Day offer an opportunity for a series on "Good Homemaking."

The local church and denominational calendars add a third level of possibilities for planned preaching. During the year sermons may be needed for the Lord's Supper, baptism, missions emphasis, ordination, stewardship, and revival preparation. The schedule will also include Sundays for special musical presentations and worship led by the youth, laity, and guest preachers.

Plan a schedule which includes preaching through books of the Bible interspersed with themes from the Christian year and the calendar. With all these possibilities fifty-two Sundays will soon be covered. In one of my pastorates, a year's pulpit work followed this plan. The first five Sundays included a series of ten messages from Philippians. February brought a series on 1 Peter. The first Sunday in March featured a mission message related to the home missions emphasis in the church. The other three Sunday mornings in March were devoted to stewardship messages. This emphasis came at the halfway point of the budget year and provided a reminder of the church's opportunities and obligations. The emphasis also tied in with a capital needs campaign for future facilities.

Sunday evenings in March–April focused on 1 Thessalonians. Morning worship in April had a series on "Faces about the Cross," leading up to Easter.

From Mother's Day through Father's Day a series of messages on the home included these titles and texts: "Living at Home during the Storm" (Matt. 7:24–27); "A Great Woman" (2 Kings 4:8–26); "Good Things That Make a Bad Marriage" (Rom. 14:16); "More Good Things That Make a Bad

Marriage," and "Good Gifts From Father" (Matt. 7:9–11). Two suicides in a local middle school and the suicide of a high school friend of our youth group lead to the message, "The Will to Live," based on Galatians 6:1–10.

The summer months included a series from 2 Thessalonians and eight sermons on prayer. With the beginning of school and an emphasis on Bible study, I preached eleven messages from Colossians centered on the preeminence of Christ and our commitment to become like Him. One of the messages used as a text was the life verse for a new minister of education and was related to his call and installation.

Two outreach/ministry projects of the church gave an opportunity for special occasion messages. On the Sunday before a downtown festival called "Light Up Orlando," I preached the message "Celebrate the Light." One purpose of the sermon called the members to involvement in the witness efforts the church would sponsor during the festival. Our involvement with the homeless elicited the message, "A People Who Rebuild," Isaiah 58:6–12; Luke 10:25–37. The message also appealed for support of a community coalition for the homeless.

December began with a world mission emphasis and continued with Christmas theme messages. Musical programs involved two evening services. At one of those I shared a brief monologue on Joseph. Dramatic effect and interest increased by doing it in a manger scene and sitting on a bale of hay.

A review of this particular year shows a scarcity of Old Testament texts. Plans were altered to meet current needs such as the message on suicide. Other messages were easily adapted to fit a special occasion. The year included a blend of Christian year themes, Bible book series, church, and denominational concerns.

REACTION AND RESPONSE

Study pages 11–36, "Planned Preaching," Martin Thielen, *Getting Ready for Sunday's Sermon* (Nashville: Broadman, 1990).

Chapter 24
Retaining Resources and Recycling Results

A series of messages on the family illustrate how the product of the study and pulpit can be used again. After first preaching them in our church, they were summarized and taped for a weekly radio devotional program sponsored by the ministerial association. An edited version was published in the *Zondervan Pastor's Annual*. In an overseas mission assignment, the director of the media center asked me to prepare Bible background material and some illustrations on the family as a resource for their Filipino radio preacher. The previously used manuscripts were easily revised, and cultural examples were added. One of the young fathers heard about that material and asked me to lead a Sunday evening family conference for couples in the church. From the material, I drafted an outline for our discussions. Some of the sermons were updated with fresh illustrations and preached in other pastorates. Recycling your messages is a legitimate way to save time and increase the value of your preparation.

RETAINING RESOURCES

Improved preaching results from the full use of the resources within your study. You will also be able to recycle the best of your previous work if you can find it. The efficient use of your study resources depends on some organization to retain and retrieve information. I have consumed valuable time trying to locate a story I remembered reading but failed to record where it was found.

Books in your personal library should be numbered, either with the Dewey Decimal System (DDS) used in most libraries or some personally devised system. I use the DDS, which groups books in like categories. Many volumes include the reference number on the publisher's information page. A booklet on the DDS religious section can be purchased, or a local library might let you copy the religious section listing.

Plan for the future when you first read a book. My book marker is a blank piece of paper with the book name and reference number at the top. As I read I note the subject and page number of an illustration or comment I want to remember. When the book is completed, the spine number and page can be noted on a subject file. Haddon Robinson's book, *Biblical Sermons,* has a spine number of 251Rob2. On page 31 of the volume is a message on adultery. The subject file listing, "Adultery," contains among its references this reference, 251Rob2/31. This sermon resource could also be referenced in the Scripture file under Exodus 20:14. Computer software and a scanner now enable you to copy printed illustrations onto an illustration disk.

Some pastors use a general file for magazine articles, newspaper clippings, conference notes, and other materials. These items can be stapled on 8 1/2 X 11 paper, if they are smaller than that size, numbered consecutively, and filed twenty-five to a folder. A general file requires periodic purging, or it will accumulate much outdated material. Whenever you add material, check existing material under that subject. If the older reference is no longer useful, just assign that number to the new article and trash the dated material. This retains a manageable size for the general file and gives it a contemporary flavor. Several brief illustrations and comments on the same subject can be placed on the same general file page. For areas which seem to generate more interest and material, you could have a separate folder numbered. This would eliminate looking for ten separate listings on the family; all of them would be found under one number.

A Scripture file contains listings for each book of the Bible. Small books may be referenced by each chapter. This file can be checked to see what the study contains on a particular passage that is the focus of your sermon preparation. Of course, general commentaries and an entire volume which covers a single subject, such as "The Holy Spirit," would not need to be referenced on the Scripture file.

This system works for some pastors. Find out what method other preachers use. You will need to determine the best organization of your resources. Begin now and maintain access to the valuable material found in your study. Computers now facilitate this process of retaining and retrieving resources, and we now turn to that subject.

Uses of the Computer

Preparation of this text has been my first major project on the computer. The more I work with the equipment, the more convinced I am of its helpfulness. A few years back I purchased an entire system: central processing unit, keyboard, terminal, printer, floppy disks, and a big box of paper. I still have half the paper! I found the manuals difficult to understand and the equipment intimidating. Much of the reason for the low usage can be traced to lack of training, failure to work alongside someone with experience until I learned the basics, and refusal to take the time necessary to learn.

A computer can be helpful in the preaching ministry but be sure you move slowly in deciding on the kind of equipment you buy. Make the decision on the basis of what you want to accomplish. Talk with pastors who use a computer and learn from them the advantages and problems. A wide variety of equipment is on the market, suitable for your needs and pocketbook. Saving a little longer for a more useful unit may pay off in the long run. Kenneth Bedell[1] suggests three steps before getting into computers: (1) identify the areas where the computer can contribute, (2) evaluate the equipment and decide which will meet your need, and (3) understand the programs used by the computer and know how to secure and evaluate programs you can use.

Before we look at some of the uses of the computer, let's review some basic terminology:

> **Central Processing Unit:** The "brains" of the system; here is contained the electronic circuits which operate the computer.
> **Terminal:** A keyboard attached to a screen used to place information into the computer. Some terminals can be secured to handle Greek and Hebrew. There is a choice of color or black and white screen display.
> **Memory:** Where the information is stored, measured in bytes. Personal computer units are designed to hold millions of pieces of input. One page of double-spaced typed material would consume 4–5,000 bytes.
> **RAM** (Random Access Memory): This memory-holding tank can be filled with information by the user and changed.
> **ROM** (Read Only Memory): This memory has set content that can't be changed. This information contains instructions which make the computer accomplish the tasks you ask it to do. The ROM content can't be lost when the computer is turned off; RAM content can be lost during a power failure or by your mistake.
> **Disk:** Floppy disks, normally of two sizes, used to store information. Information you have placed on the RAM can be saved on a disk. One 3 1/2" disk contains the entire text of this book.

CD-ROM: A compact disk unit which attaches to your personal computer and is capable of holding much more data.

Printer: A unit to print the material you have prepared on the computer. Varieties include a dot-matrix, which prints with a series of dots; letter quality; or laser printer, which provides the best quality of printing.

Modem: Equipment used to transfer information from one computer to another, usually through a telephone line.

Software: Instructions that program the computer to do tasks you desire. These instructions are on a disk and come with a manual. You download (or move the information from the disk) to the RAM.

Many accessories are available for other uses.

Uses of the Computer in Preaching

Government and business now use computers in all phases of their work. Most libraries are moving to computerization. An increasing number of churches, large and small, have discovered the practical uses of computers. Your church may already be using a computer to track financial records and prepare reports. Software for membership services and desktop publishing are widely used. A county fair included a church exhibit utilizing a computer to answer questions people punched in about the denomination.

Word processing, filing, and securing additional information will probably be the major uses of a computer for the preaching ministry. Once you use computer word processing, you'll not want to return to a typewriter, even a self-correcting one. With a computer, words, sentences, paragraphs, and pages of material can be added, deleted, or switched with simple commands. Errors can be quickly corrected before the final copy is printed. Underlining, italics, indenting, bold type, single or double spacing can all be accomplished with ease, and if you don't like the way it looks on the screen, you can change it back just as easily.

Computer resources can help us understand the text with the use of Bible study software. Many programs contain a basic pastor's study. The vast amount of material requires a CD-ROM drive attached to your personal computer. One compact disk includes texts of the Greek New Testament, two Greek lexicons, the one volume *Theological Dictionary of the New Testament*, four English translations of the Bible, three Bible commentaries, two Bible dictionaries, and other features.

Other programs feature concordances which enable you to do word studies. Some software include definitions and also have the capacity to enter your own sermon study notes and keep them for later recall. *Christian Computing* magazine is published eleven times each year and includes reviews of new Christian software, study helps, and Christian sites on the Internet. Preaching journals regularly update subscribers on the latest technology resources that support sermon preparation.

The computer can replace the paper filing system earlier described. Scripture, sermon, and illustration files can all be maintained on disks. You can compose the forms that will be most useful to you. Illustrations can be coded with a key word, and, when that word is entered, the computer will bring up every illustration stored under that heading. Electronic scanners are now available which read printed text and record it on the computer.

With a modem, your personal computer can be connected to libraries and Internet information services and tremendously expand your source for support material. Some of these services carry a subscription fee and line usage charge.

Remember This!

I still vividly remember the day I worked on the computer for two hours and had to do it all over. Save often! Some units are programmed to remind you every two pages, "Save Now?" An excellent idea! Make a duplicate copy of material you desire to keep, in case something happens to the disk you are working with. Put a static pad under the computer to prevent static electricity from wiping out data. A friend recently warned us in the office not to lay a disk on the drive unit; it can cause a loss of material. Avoid low humidity in the room where the unit is stored. A power surge plug helps prevent damage caused by fluctuation of the current, or a surge when loss of power is restored.[2]

Michael Duduit noted, "The church cannot escape the computer era—nor should we want to try! Computers are like pencil, paper and books—they are tools to help us work more effectively."[3]

RECYCLING RESULTS

With an organized study and consistent study habits, your own material will begin to grow. A sermon prepared for your pastorate has potential for wider usage. Recycling has become a national concern to conserve natural resources. Why not conserve the results of your preparation?

When can you preach a sermon the second time in your church? I once heard George Buttrick respond, "Change the illustrations and preach it that night." That certainly speaks to the power of effective illustrations and may describe the retention of our members. Noted Australian preacher F. W. Boreham, 1871–1959, used an unusual technique throughout his ministry. He prepared "only one new sermon a week, and for the other service he would recast and revise one that he had previously delivered."[4]

Some pastors have an announced "Preach It Again" month. Members indicate their favorite sermon preached during the preceeding months and the "top four" are featured during the month.

As glass bottles are melted down and reformed into useful products, your older sermons can be preached with a different structure. A sermon on Romans 5:1–5, which I had used many times, became two messages. With a little work the original could be expanded to a four message series on "Amazing Grace." Bible personality sermons can be restructured as a monologue. Restyle a deductive sermon into an inductive approach. With the Bible study already completed, devote available time to creative brainstorming on the older manuscript. The result might be a more appealing title, an intriguing thesis sentence, fresh illustrations, leaner major divisions. Automobile companies retain a chassis for several years and restyle the body. Try that approach on sermons in your file.

Radio offers an outlet for recycling your preaching. Many communities have a daily devotional time. A member asked me why I couldn't do at church what happened on the radio: a twenty-five minute sermon in eight minutes! Consider more creative use of radio time, such as thirty-to-forty-five-second spots run at peak listening slots. These would cost more but probably reach more people. Glean your sermons for powerful illustrations and incisive comments which drive home a biblical truth. These spots can hook the interest of a fast-paced society. A friend of mine has a weekly commentary, applying Scripture to current events, on a popular radio talk show. Similar opportunities are available with some television stations, especially small-town cable companies. Ralph Duncan pastored a church three miles from a town of 2,000. Attendance of his church averaged about 125, but Duncan's ministry reached into several counties to thousands of people. Using the central idea of a sermon and a key illustration, he developed an expanded ministry through radio and print. He prepared a three-to-four-minute broadcast which aired on four stations covering three counties and reaching into four other counties. The program scripts were edited slightly and sent to seven newspapers for weekly publication. Circulation of the seven newspapers totaled thirty thousand with a potential readership of nearly one hundred thousand. Photocopies of the newspaper columns later appeared on the back of the Sunday bulletin and as inserts in mail-outs.

Many of Duncan's articles were "straight out of the pulpit," and focused on social/ethical concerns from a biblical perspective. The writer received letters from people in six states and long distance calls about his material. Duncan observed, "Every preacher tells stories and can usually write them. If he can't write them, he should learn how to write better. A focus on personal experience tied to Scripture will speak to people."[5]

Retaining Resources and Recycling Results

Preaching journals, devotional booklets, and Sunday school curriculum are other outlets for expanding the results of your preaching study. Some denominations provide writer's conferences to guide would-be authors in preparation of specific writing assignments. Some materials I have written for publication were edited from sermons; other material was prepared for publication and later preached.

I certainly hope you have not misinterpreted my emphasis on recycling your messages as an encouragement not to study and prepare new sermons. Some preachers "pull out of the barrel" filled during their first pastorate and prepare little new material. This soon kills creativity and robs a church from hearing a "Word from the Lord" given just for them. Previously prepared material should receive a good reworking, considering the needs of the current situation, contemporary illustrations, and relevant application. Adequate preparation time in a well-organized study helps make this possible.

REACTION AND RESPONSE

If you are not using a computer in your preaching ministry, talk with some preachers who do and consider how your preparation and resources could be helped by technology.

Endnotes

Chapter One

1. Robert H. Mounce, *The Essential Nature of New Testament Preaching* (Grand Rapids: Wm. B. Eerdmans Publishing Co., 1960), 17–18.
2. Ibid., 42–43.

Chapter Two

1. Raymond Bailey, *Jesus the Preacher* (Nashville: Broadman Press, 1990), 12.

Chapter Three

1. H. C. Brown Jr., Gordon Clinard, and Jesse Northcutt, *Steps to the Sermon* (Nashville: Broadman Press, 1963), 9.
2. Clyde Fant, *Preaching for Today* (New York: Harper & Row, 1975), 26.
3. Mounce, *New Testament Preaching*, 152.
4. Ibid., 154.
5. William J. Reynolds, "Share His Love" (Nashville: Broadman Press, 1973).
6. George Atkins, "Brethren, We Have Met to Worship."

Chapter Four

1. John R. W. Stott, *The Preacher's Portrait* (Grand Rapids: Eerdmans, 1961), 74.
2. Clyde F. Fant Jr. and William M. Pinson Jr., *20 Centuries of Great Preaching* (Waco: Word, 1971), 9:315.
3. Mounce, *New Testament Preaching*, 158.
4. Stott, *The Preacher's Portrait*, 31.

5. Ibid., 76.
6. Catherine Marshall, *A Man Called Peter* (New York: McGraw-Hill, 1952), 43.

CHAPTER FIVE
1. Bailey, *Jesus the Preacher*, 23.
2. Stott, *The Preacher's Portrait*, 22.
3. Fant and Pinson, *20 Centuries*, 12:299.
4. R. Albert Mohler Jr., "A Theology of Preaching," in *Handbook of Contemporary Preaching*, ed. Michael Duduit (Nashville: Broadman & Holman, 1992), 15.

CHAPTER SIX
1. Jeffrey J. Mayer, *If You Haven't Got the Time to Do It Right, When Will You Find the Time to Do It Over?* (New York: Simon and Schuster, 1991).

CHAPTER EIGHT
1. George E. Sweazey, *Preaching the Good News* (Englewood Cliffs, N.J.: Prentice Hall, 1976), 31.
2. Dean Dickens, *How to Preach* (Davao City, Philippines: PhilBEST, 1984), 18.
3. John A. Broadus, *On the Preparation and Delivery of Sermons*, rev. J. B. Weatherspoon (Nashville: Broadman Press, 1944), 25.
4. Fant and Pinson, *20 Centuries*, 9:133.
5. Fant, *Preaching for Today*, 103.
6. Mounce, *New Testament Preaching*, 156.

CHAPTER NINE
1. John R. W. Stott, *Between Two Worlds: The Art of Preaching in the Twentieth Century* (Grand Rapids: Eerdmans, 1982), 137.
2. Farrar Patterson, *Do-It-Yourself Bible Study: The Inductive Method* (Fort Worth: Latimer House, 1985), 7.
3. John C. Cooper, author's written notes, February 20, 1995.
4. Wayne McDill, *The 12 Essential Skills for Great Preaching* (Nashville: Broadman & Holman, 1994), 27.
5. Ibid., 13.
6. Ibid., 25, 27.
7. W. E. Vine, Merrill F. Unger, and William White Jr., eds., *Vine's Expository Dictionary of Biblical Words* (Nashville: Thomas Nelson, 1985), 283.
8. George A. Buttrick, *The Parables of Jesus* (Grand Rapids: Baker, 1973), xv.

Endnotes

CHAPTER ELEVEN

1. J. H. Jowett, *The Preacher: His Life and Work* (New York: G. H. Doran, 1912), 133.
2. Broadus, *Preparation and Delivery*, 37.
3. Fant and Pinson, *20 Centuries*, 9:48–50.
4. Ibid., 8:77.
5. T. T. Crabtree, *The Zondervan 1984 Pastor's Annual* (Grand Rapids: Zondervan, 1983), 127–129.
6. Warren W. Wiersbe, *Be Rich* (Wheaton, Ill.: Victor Books, 1983), 29.
7. Jowett, *The Preacher*, 133.
8. Bill Hybels, Stuart Briscoe, and Haddon Robinson, *Mastering Contemporary Preaching* (Portland: Multnomah Press, 1989), 32.

CHAPTER TWELVE

1. *Proclaim*, 21, no. 4 (1991): 5.
2. Fant, *Preaching for Today*, 137–138.

CHAPTER THIRTEEN

1. Broadus, *Preparation and Delivery*, 93.
2. W. E. Sangster, *The Craft of the Sermon* (London: Epworth, 1954), 90.
3. Manuel Scott, Ky. Pastor's Conference, n.d.
4. Fant and Pinson, *20 Centuries*, 9:214.
5. James E. Stewart, *The Wind of the Spirit* (Nashville: Abingdon, 1968), 9.
6. Andrew W. Blackwood, *Doctrinal Preaching for Today*, n.p., n.d.
7. Fant and Pinson, *20 Centuries*, 11:131.
8. Fred B. Craddock, *As One without Authority* (Nashville: Abingdon, 1979), 52.
9. Ralph L. Lewis with Gregg Lewis, *Inductive Preaching: Helping People Listen* (Westchester, Ill: Crossway Books, 1983), 165.
10. Broadus, *Preparation and Delivery*, 141–154.
11. Craddock, *As One without Authority*, 53.

CHAPTER FOURTEEN

1. V. L. Stanfield, *Evangelistic Preaching*, n.p., n.d., 67.
2. Fant and Pinson, *20 Centuries*, 8:227.
3. Broadus, *Preparation and Delivery*, 122.
4. Fant and Pinson, *20 Centuries*, 12:325.
5. Paul Scherer, *The Word God Sent* (New York: Harper & Row, 1965), 204.
6. Crabtree, *Pastor's Annual*, 339.
7. Stewart, *The Wind of the Spirit*, 123.

Chapter Fifteen

1. Greg Stoda, "Hogan's World at 78: Simple and Small," *Lexington Herald-Leader,* 23 July 1991.
2. Fant and Pinson, *20 Centuries,* 12:150.
3. Ibid., 10:200.
4. Ibid., 6:249.
5. James C. Barry, "An Interview with Clyde Fant," *Search,* 16, no. 2 (1986): 56.
6. Ibid., 50.

Chapter Sixteen

1. Brian L. Harbour, "Concluding the Sermon," ed. Michael Duduit, *Handbook of Contemporary Preaching,* 270.
2. Stott, *Between Two Worlds,* 144.
3. Fant and Pinson, *20 Centuries,* 10:104.
4. Jim Lowery, "Preaching Must Mix Then and Now," *Facts and Trends* 28, no. 10 (1984).
5. Scherer, *The Word God Sent,* 78.
6. Fant and Pinson, *20 Centuries,* 11:188.
7. Ibid., 10:11.
8. Lowery, "Preaching Must Mix."
9. Hybels, Briscoe, and Robinson, *Mastering Contemporary Preaching,* 65.

Chapter Seventeen

1. James E. Hightower, *Illustrating Paul's Letter to the Romans* (Nashville: Broadman Press, 1984), 8.
2. Brown, Clinard, and Northcutt, *Steps to the Sermon,* 79.
3. Fant and Pinson, *20 Centuries,* 11:339.
4. Marjorie Rawlings, *The Yearling* (New York: Charles Scribner's, 1939), 200.
5. D. L. Lowrie, sermon, Clear Creek Baptist Bible College, August 6, 1991.
6. Adapted from a story in *Pacific Stars and Stripes* (22 April 1984).
7. Adapted from a story in *Asiaweek* (15 July 1983).
8. Fant and Pinson, *20 Centuries,* 10:13.
9. William Manchester, *The Last Lion: Winston Spencer Churchill; 1932–1940* (New York: Bantam Doubleday Dell, 1988), 350.
10. Hightower, *Paul's Letter,* 115.
11. Madame Guyon, *Union with God* (Augusta, Maine: Christian Books, 1981), 97.
12. Hybels, Briscoe, and Robinson, *Mastering Contemporary Preaching,* 36.

Endnotes

13. Hightower, *Paul's Letter*, 98.
14. Mariah Carey, "There's Got to Be a Way," (New York: CBS Records, Inc., 1990).
15. Crabtree, *Pastor's Annual*, 332.
16. Calvin Miller, "Call in the Witnesses," *Proclaim* 28, no. 4 (1999): 4–7.
17. Hybels, Briscoe, and Robinson, *Mastering Contemporary Preaching*, 139.

CHAPTER EIGHTEEN
1. Lew Wallace, *Ben Hur* (Pleasantville, N.Y.: The Reader's Digest Association, 1992), 52.
2. *Desk Standard Dictionary* (Funk & Wagnalls, n.d.)
3. Broadus, *Preparation and Delivery*, 279.
4. Ibid., 284.
5. Ibid., 285.
6. Ibid., 286–292.
7. Stott, *Between Two Worlds*, 238.

CHAPTER NINETEEN
1. Stephen Olford, *Annointed Expository Preaching* (Nashville: Broadman & Holman, 1998), 343.
2. Walter J. Burghardt, "A Kind of Loving, for Me" in *Best Sermons 4*, ed. James Cox, (San Francisco: Harper, 1991), 145.
3. Bill D. Whittaker, *Award Winning Sermons*, vol. 4 (Nashville: Broadman Press, 1980), 106–110.
4. John Dart, "Whatever Happened to Hell?" The *Courier-Journal*, 24 September 1978.
5. Atkins, "Brethren, We Have Met to Worship."
6. Haddon W. Robinson, *Biblical Sermons* (Grand Rapids: Baker, 1989), 43.
7. Hybels, Briscoe, and Robinson, *Mastering Contemporary Preaching*, 58.

CHAPTER TWENTY
1. Michael Duduit, *Handbook of Contemporary Preaching* (Nashville: Broadman & Holman, n.d.), 93.
2. Blackwood, *Doctrinal Preaching*, 87.
3. Ibid, 89.
4. Jay E. Adams, *Truth Applied* (Grand Rapids: Zondervan, 1990), 41.
5. Whittaker, *Award Winning Sermons*, vol. 3 (Nashville: Broadman Press, 1979), 61.

6. Whittaker, *Sermons*, vol. 4, 113.
7. Ibid., 119.

CHAPTER TWENTY-ONE
1. Hybels, Briscoe, Robinson, *Mastering Contemporary Preaching*, 81.
2. "The Principle of Life," *Proclaim*, March 1996, 31–32.

CHAPTER TWENTY-TWO
1. Franklin Segler, *A Theology of Church and Ministry* (Nashville: Broadman Press, 1960), 23.
2. Fant and Pinson, *20 Centuries*, 10:11
3. Holmes and Rahe, "Stress Test For Adults," 1977.
4. Harold T. Bryson, *Building Sermons to Meet People's Needs* (Nashville: Broadman Press, 1980), 41.
5. Fant, *Preaching for Today*, 51.
6. Lloyd M. Perry, *Biblical Preaching for Today's World* (Chicago: Moody Press, 1990), 152–153.
7. John A. Huffman in *Inside The Sermon,* ed. Richard Bodey (New York: Harper & Row, 1990), 143–150.
8. Charles L. Quarles, International Mission Board Seminary Professor, sermon, Romania, n.d.
9. Halford E. Luccock, *Communicating the Gospel* (New York: Harper Bros., 1954), 85.

CHAPTER TWENTY-THREE
1. George Gibson, *Planned Preaching* (Philadelphia: The Westminster Press, 1954), 14.
2. John Killinger, *Fundamentals of Preaching* (Fortress Press, 1989), 167.
3. Robinson, *Biblical Sermons*, 11.
4. Andrew W. Blackwood, *Expository Preaching for Today* (Grand Rapids: Baker, 1975), 175.
5. J. Winston Pearce, *Planning Your Preaching* (Nashville: Broadman Press, 1967), 5.
6. Ibid.
7. Hybels, Briscoe, and Robinson, *Mastering Contemporary Preaching,* 161–162.
8. Blackwood, *Doctrinal Preaching,* 175.
9. Ibid.
10. Harold Bryson, *Expository Preaching: The Art of Preaching through a Book of the Bible* (Nashville: Broadman & Holman, 1995).

Endnotes

11. Blackwood, *Doctrinal Preaching*, 171.
12. Chip Alford, "Sermon Planning Relieves Stress, Conference Leader Tells Pastors," *Florida Baptist Witness* (17 October 1991): 16.

CHAPTER TWENTY-FOUR

1. Kenneth Bedell, *Using Personal Computers in the Church* (Valley Forge: Judson Press, 1982), 8.
2. Russell H. Dilday Jr., *Personal Computer: A New Tool for Ministers* (Nashville: Broadman Press, 1982), 68.
3. Michael Duduit, "Using Your Computer in Sermon Preparation," *Preaching* 6, no. 2 (September 1991).
4. Fant and Pinson, *20 Centuries*, 8:192.
5. Ralph Duncan, interview by author, Springfield Baptist Church, Bimble, Ky., 21 November 1991.

Bibliography

Adams, Jay. *Preaching with Purpose*. Grand Rapids: Baker Book House, 1982.
Adams, Jay E. *Truth Applied*. Grand Rapids: Zondervan, 1990.
Alford, Chip. "Sermon Planning Relieves Stress, Conference Leader Tells Pastors." *Florida Baptist Witness,* 17 October 1991.
Award Winning Sermons. Nashville: Broadman Press, 1979.
Bailey, Raymond. *Jesus the Preacher*. Nashville: Broadman Press, 1990.
———. *Paul the Preacher*. Nashville: Broadman Press, 1991.
Baumann, J. Daniel. *An Introduction to Contemporary Preaching*. Grand Rapids: Baker, 1988.
Bedell, Kenneth. *Using Personal Computers in the Church*. Valley Forge: Judson Press, 1982.
Bennett, Bill. *Thirty Minutes to Raise the Dead: How You Can Preach Your Best Sermon Yet—This Sunday*. Nashville: Thomas Nelson Publishers, 1991.
Biblical Preaching: An Expositor's Treasury. Edited by James W. Cox Philadelphia: The Westminster Press, 1983.
Blackwood, Andrew W. *Doctrinal Preaching for Today*. N.p., n.d.
———. *Expository Preaching for Today*. Grand Rapids: Baker, 1975.
———. *Planning a Year's Pulpit Work*. Nashville: Abingdon, 1952.
———. *The Preparation of Sermons*. New York: Abingdon-Cokesbury, 1958.
Inside the Sermon: Thirteen Preachers Discuss Their Methods of Preparing Messages. Edited by Richard Allen Bodey. Grand Rapids: Baker, 1990.
Bodey, Richard. *Inside the Sermon*. New York: Harper & Row, 1990.
Braga, James. *How to Prepare Bible Messages*. Portland: Multnomah, 1982.
Broadus, John A. *On the Preparation and Delivery of Sermons*. Revised by J. B. Weatherspoon. Nashville: Broadman Press, 1944.

Brown, H. C. *A Quest for Reformation in Preaching.* Waco, Tex.: Word Books, 1968.

Brown, H. C. Jr., H. Gordon Clinard, and Jesse J. Northcutt. *Steps to the Sermon.* Nashville: Broadman Press, 1963.

Bryson, Harold T. *Expository Preaching: The Art of Preaching through a Book of the Bible.* Nashville: Broadman & Holman, 1995.

Bryson, Harold T,. and James C. Taylor. *Building Sermons to Meet People's Needs.* Nashville: Broadman Press, 1980.

Burghardt, Walter J. "A Kind of Loving, for Me." In *Best Sermons 4,* edited by James Cox. San Francisco: Harper, 1991.

Buttrick, George A. *The Parables of Jesus.* Grand Rapids: Baker, 1973.

Chartier, Myron, R. *Preaching as Communication.* Nashville: Abingdon, 1981.

Crabtree, T. T. *The Zondervan 1984 Pastor's Annual.* Grand Rapids: Zondervan, 1983.

Craddock, Fred B. *As One without Authority.* Nashville: Abingdon, 1979.

———. *Preaching.* Nashville: Abingdon Press, 1985.

Dart, John. "Whatever Happened to Hell?" The *Courier-Journal,* 24 September 1978.

Davis, H. Grady. *Design for Preaching.* Philadelphia: Fortress, 1958.

Dickens, Dean. *How to Preach.* Davao City, Philippines: PhilBest, 1984.

Drakeford, John W. *Humor in Preaching.* Grand Rapids: Zondervan, 1986.

Duduit, Michael. *Handbook of Contemporary Preaching.* Nashville: Broadman & Holman, 1992.

Duncan, Ralph. Interview by author. Springfield Baptist Church, Bimble, Ky., 21 November 1991.

Fant, Clyde E. *Preaching for Today.* New York: Harper & Row, 1977.

Fant, Clyde F. Jr., and William M. Pinson, Jr. *20 Centuries of Great Preaching.* Waco: Word, 1971.

Forbes, James. *The Holy Spirit and Preaching.* Nashville: Abingdon, 1989.

Gibson, George. *Planned Preaching.* Philadelphia: The Westminster Press, 1954.

Guyon, Madame. *Union with God.* Augusta, Maine: Christian Books, 1981.

Hall, E. Eugene, and James L. Heflin. *Proclaim the Word!* Nashville: Broadman, 1985.

Harbour, Brian L. "Concluding the Sermon." In *Handbook of Contemporary Preaching,* edited by Michael Duduit. Nashville: Broadman & Holman, 1992.

Hightower, James E. *Illustrating Paul's Letter to the Romans.* Nashville: Broadman Press, 1984.

Huffman, John A. In *Inside the Sermon,* edited by Richard Bodey. New York: Harper & Row, 1990.

Hybels, Bill, Stuart Briscoe, and Haddon Robinson. *Mastering Contemporary Preaching.* Portland: Multomah, 1989.

Bibliography

Jones, Ilian T. *Principles and Practice of Preaching.* Nashville: Abingdon, 1956.
Jowett, J. H. *The Preacher: His Life and Work.* New York: G. H. Doran, 1912.
Killinger, John. *Fundamentals of Preaching.* Philadelphia: Fortress Press, 1989.
Kooienga, William H. *Elements of Style for Preaching.* Grand Rapids: Zondervan, 1989.
Lewis, Ralph L., and Gregg Lewis. *Inductive Preaching: Helping People Listen.* Westchester, Ill.: Crossway Books, 1982.
Lloyd-Jones, D. Martyn. *Preaching and Preachers.* Grand Rapids: Zondervan, 1971.
Loccock, Halford E. *Communicating the Gospel.* New York: Harper Bros., 1954.
Long, Thomas G., and Neely Dixon McCarter. *Preaching In and Out of Season.* Louisville: Westminster/John Knox, 1990.
Loscalzo, Craig A. *Preaching Sermons That Connect.* Downers Grove, Ill.: Intervarsity, 1992.
Lowery, Jim. "Preaching Must Mix Then and Now." *Facts and Trends,* 1984.
Luccock, Halford E. *Communicating the Gospel.* New York: Harper and Row, 1990.
MacArthur, John Jr. and the Master's Seminary Faculty. *Rediscovering Expository Preaching.* Dallas: Word, 1992.
Manchester, William. *The Last Lion: Winston Spencer Churchill; 1932–1940.* New York: Bantam Doubleday Dell, 1988.
Marshall, Catherine. *A Man Called Peter.* New York: McGraw-Hill, 1952.
Mawhinney, Bruce. *Preaching with Freshness.* Eugene, Ore.: Harvest Home, 1991.
Mayer, Jeffrey J. *If You Haven't Got the Time to Do It Right, When Will You Find the Time to Do It Over?* New York: Simon and Schuster, 1991.
McDill, Wayne. *The 12 Essential Skills for Great Preaching.* Nashville: Broadman & Holman, 1994.
Meyer, F. B. *Expository Preaching: Plans and Methods.* New York: George H. Doran, 1912.
Miller, Calvin. *Spirit, Word, and Story: A Philosophy of Preaching.* Dallas: Word, 1989.
———. "Call in the Witnesses." *Proclaim* 28:4, 1999.
Mohler, R. Albert, Jr. "A Theology of Preaching." In *Handbook of Contemporary Preaching,* edited by Michael Duduit. Nashville: Broadman & Holman, 1992.
Mounce, Robert H. *The Essentials of New Testament Preaching.* Grand Rapids: Eerdmans, 1960.
Olford, David L., comp. *A Passion for Preaching: Reflections on the Art of Preaching.* Nashville: Thomas Nelson Publishers, 1989.
Olford, Stephen L., with David L. Olford. *Annointed Expository Preaching.* Nashville: Broadman & Holman, 1998.

Patterson, Farrar. *Do-It-Yourself Bible Study: The Inductive Method.* Fort Worth: Latimer House, 1985.
Pearce, J. Winston. *Planning Your Preaching.* Nashville: Broadman, 1967.
Perry, Lloyd M. *Biblical Preaching for Today's World.* Chicago: Moody Press, 1973.
Pitt-Watson, Ian. *A Primer for Preachers.* Nashville: Broadman, 1967.
Proclaim, 21:4, 1991.
Proclaim, March 1996.
Rawlings, Marjorie. *The Yearling.* New York: Charles Scribner's, 1939.
Read, David H. C. *Preaching about the Needs of Real People.* Philadelphia: The Westminster Press, 1988.
Reynolds, William J. "Share His Love." Nashville: Broadman, 1973.
Robinson, Haddon W. *Biblical Preaching.* Grand Rapids: Baker, 1980.
———. *Biblical Sermons.* Grand Rapids: Baker, 1989.
Roddy, Clarence S. *We Prepare and Preach.* Chicago: Moody Press, 1959.
Sangster, W. E. *The Craft of the Sermon.* London: Epworth, 1954.
Scherer, Paul. *The Word God Sent.* New York: Harper & Row. 1965.
Search, 16:2, 1986.
Segler, Franklin. *A Theology of Church and Ministry.* Nashville: Broadman, 1960.
Stanfield, V. L. *Evangelistic Preaching.* N.p., n.d.
Stewart, James E. *The Wind of the Spirit.* Nashville: Abingdon, 1968.
Stoda, Greg. "Hogan's World at 78: Simple and Small." *Lexington Herald Leader.* 23 July 1991.
Stott, John R. W. *Between Two Worlds: The Art of Preaching in the Twentieth Century.* Grand Rapids: Eerdmans, 1982.
———. *The Preacher's Portrait.* Grand Rapids: Eerdmans, 1961.
Sweazey, George E. *Preaching the Good News.* New Jersey: Prentice Hall, 1976.
Thielen, Martin. *Getting Ready for Sunday's Sermons: A Practical Guide for Sermon Preparation.* Nashville: Broadman, 1990.
Unger, Merrill F. *Principles of Expository Preaching.* Grand Rapids: Zondervan, 1982.
Vine, W. E., Merrill F. Unger, and William White Jr., eds. *Vine's Expository Dictionary of Biblical Words.* Nashville: Thomas Nelson Publishers, 1985.
Wallace, Lew. *Ben Hur.* Pleasantville, N.Y.: The Reader's Digest Association, 1992.
Wiersbe, Warren W. *Preaching and Teaching with Imagination: The Quest for Biblical Ministry.* Wheaton, Ill.: Victor Books, 1994.
———. *Be Rich.* Wheaton, Ill.: Victor Books, 1983.
Whittaker, Bill D. *Award Winning Sermons.* Vol. 3. Nashville: Broadman, 1979.
———. *Award Winning Sermons.* Vol. 4. Nashville: Broadman, 1980.

Clear Creek Baptist Bible College

Clear Creek Baptist Bible College exists to provide educational preparation for adults called of God into Christian service. Located in Pineville, Kentucky, in the picturesque Appalachian mountains, Clear Creek grants a one-year certificate, two-year associate degree, three-year diploma, and a four-year Bachelor of Arts in Ministry degree. At Clear Creek, every student majors in Bible and can train for ministry. The college places an emphasis on adults, with an average student age of thirty-one. Many are married with children. An open admissions policy allows students to complete GED requirements during their first year at Clear Creek. A campus workship program is available for students and their spouses. Clear Creek has low tuition and reasonable housing costs.

ADMISSIONS

Admission into Clear Creek focuses on your goal of serving the Lord through your faithfulness to his "call." Every student in the program states clearly the call to serve the Lord in ministry. Your background is important to us because it helps define what strengths and skills you bring to our Clear Creek classrooms.

Academic history plays an important role in helping the college assess your needs as you direct your energy toward preparation for the ministry. Many students bring secular skills to Clear Creek, and 51 percent have prior college credits. Preparation for God's service is our goal. No matter what your previous educational accomplishments, we offer the resources to equip and prepare you to serve the Lord in ministry.

ACADEMICS

Every degree student majors in Bible. The Bachelor of Arts in Ministry offers four church-related areas of ministry: Pastoral, Church Ministries, Missions/Evangelism, and Church Music.

Our faculty brings a balance of outstanding academic credentials and practical ministry experience into the classroom. Their balanced approach to teaching provides an informed leadership model as you develop your ministry skills. God's presence and power will direct your studies because at Clear Creek, the Bible is not an ancient religious textbook. It is the inspired word of God, our unfailing and all-sufficient guide for faith and practice.

Clear Creek Baptist Bible College

CAMPUS LIFE

Clear Creek is a place for you to call home while you study and become the person God is molding, shaping, and equipping. By Jesus' example we will nurture and embrace you as the splendor and beauty of Appalachia surround you. Many of our students are refreshed while hiking, fishing, biking, and swimming on our seven-hundred-acre campus. God continues to grow our campus and we recently completed a new classroom building. The facilities at Clear Creek offer an outstanding library, family life center, medical and dental clinic, and child development center.

MINISTRY

Your hope is in the God who placed His call on your life, but we can encourage you as you develop your ministry skills. Our proven success rate demonstrates that you will be prepared. Within ninety days of graduation, 94 percent of Clear Creek graduates have been called to a ministry position or enrolled in seminary. Our singular purpose at Clear Creek is to train men and women for ministry. We want to be part of God's plan for your life.

Clear Creek Baptist Bible College
300 Clear Creek Road
Pineville, Kentucky 40977
606-337-3196
Fax: 606-337-2372
Email: ccbbc@tcnet.net
Web site: www.ccbbc.edu

Biblical Reference Index

Scriptures cited as sermon texts

Genesis
Ch. 1:26–31	162
Chs. 37–50	91

Exodus
Ch. 20:13	161
Ch. 35:20–29	101

Joshua
Ch. 3:1–4	50

1 Kings
Ch. 22:41–53	50

2 Kings
Ch. 4.8–26	79

2 Chronicles
Ch. 32:1–8	92

Proverbs
Ch. 31:10–31	50

Isaiah
Ch. 6:1–8	157
Ch. 40:31	118

Ezekiel
Ch. 37:1–11	80

Daniel
Ch. 1–3	90

Matthew
Ch. 3:13–17	93, 119
Chs. 5–7	11–12
Ch. 11:12–11	100
Ch. 25:14–20	145
Ch. 28:16–20	118
Ch. 28:18–19	93

Mark
Ch. 1:14–15	11
Ch. 2:1–12	83–87

Luke
Ch. 23:44–54	50
Ch. 24:33–35	91

John
Ch. 3:1–15	89-91
Ch. 3:8	89
Ch. 3:16	146–149
Ch. 8:31–37	50

Acts
Ch. 2:14–40	13–14
Ch. 2:36–47	146
Ch. 2:40–41	93
Ch. 7:2–53	15
Ch. 8:26–39	144
Ch. 8:26–40	76–77

Ch. 9	154	Ch. 3:12–14	169
Ch. 10:1–20	162	Ch. 4:4–7	100
Ch. 10:34–43	14	**Colossians**	
Ch. 13:16–41	16	Ch. 3:12–15	170–175
Ch. 14:8–18	92	Ch. 4:14	79
Ch. 16:25–34	145	**2 Thessalonians**	
Ch. 17:22–31	16, 117	Ch. 1:3–4	61–65, 67–69, 74
Ch. 21:1–14	48–49	**2 Timothy**	
Romans		Ch. 2:20–21	124
Ch. 3:23–25	65–66	Ch. 4:9, 21	54
Ch. 5:1–5	108–109	Ch. 4:10	79
Ch. 6:3–4	93	**Philemon**	
Ch. 13:1–7	163	Ch. 24	79
Ch. 13:11–14	57, 130	**James**	
Ch. 16:1–16	129	Ch. 1:6–7	115
1 Corinthians		**1 Peter**	
Ch. 16:1–2	119–120	Ch. 1:22–2:12	156
2 Corinthians		Ch. 2:13–17	163
Ch. 5:6–11	50	**2 Peter**	
Galatians		Ch. 1:1–11	94
Ch. 4:4–5	50	**1 John**	
Ch. 6:7–8	83	Ch. 1:8–9	110
Ephesians		Ch. 3:1–3	50
Ch. 1:15–23	80	**Revelation**	
Ch. 4:28	162	Ch. 1:17–20	155
Philippians			
Ch. 3:1–10	45		

About the Author

Billy Douglas (Bill) Whittaker, a Baptist minister and teacher, is the president of Clear Creek Baptist Bible College in Pineville, Kentucky. He was educated at Warren County High School in Bowling Green, Kentucky, and received a bachelor of arts degree from Western Kentucky University. Whittaker is a graduate of Southern Baptist Theological Seminary in Louisville, Kentucky, where he received a master of divinity and doctor of divinity degrees.

Dr. Whittaker was ordained in 1964 at Calvary Baptist Church in Bowling Green, which was also the site of his 1959 conversion. He has been pastor of Jackson Grove Baptist Church in Bowling Green; First Baptist Church in Sturgis, Kentucky; First Baptist Church in Murray, Kentucky; and Downtown Baptist Church, in Orlando, Florida. Whittaker also served as assistant to the dean of student affairs at Western Kentucky University.

As a student, Whittaker served as a student summer missionary in the Philippines. Then, in 1982, Whittaker was appointed by the Foreign Mission Board of the Southern Baptist Convention to serve as pastor of International Baptist Church in Manila. During his service there, he also served as chairman of the Manila substation of the Philippine Baptist Mission; chairman of the Camp FIMIKI committee; professor at the Southern Baptist School of Theology in Manila; instructor at the John Bisagno Manila Crusade School of Evangelism; and led in the establishment of two new churches.

Dr. Whittaker has been active in many mission and evangelism efforts. He served as a member of mission teams to Eastern Kentucky, Michigan, Ohio,

Indiana, Montana, Brazil, and Jamaica. He has attended the Baptist World Alliance, and served as a crusade evangelist in Guam, Australia, and Nigeria. In 1997 and 1999, he visited Russia and served as a teacher in pastor's schools in Tambov and Novgorod. Each year, Dr. Whittaker preaches in an average of six revivals, which in the past have included churches in Kentucky, Ohio, Indiana, Michigan, Missouri, South Carolina, and Pennsylvania. He is certified in Evangelism Explosion and Masterlife.

Whittaker has served the Kentucky Baptist Convention in numerous capacities, including the Executive Board 1971–1975 and 1977–1982. He served as president of the Convention 1980–1981, and Pastor's Conference president in 1979. He has also served as chairman of the Christian Education Depth Study, second vice-president, Committee on Credentials, and Special Bold Missions Committee.

Dr. Whittaker has also served on the Kentucky Baptist Board of Child Care, as director of the Clear Creek Baptist Bible College Christmas Project, president of the Southern Seminary Kentucky Alumni, and is a life member of the Kentucky Baptist Historical Society.

Whittaker has written extensively, and his sermons and articles have appeared in the *Western Recorder, Deacon, Proclaim, Preaching, Search*, books, annuals, and other publications. Whittaker is married to the former Rebecca Kaye Howard, also of Bowling Green. They are the parents of three children and grandparents of one.